THE CULTIVATED WILD

THE CULTIVATED WILD

GARDENS AND LANDSCAPES BY RAYMOND JUNGLES

INTRODUCTION BY CHARLES BIRNBAUM

THE MONACELLI PRESS

WILD THING, YOU MAKE MY HEART SING

CHARLES A. BIRNBAUM, FASLA, FAAR

It has been seven years since The Monacelli Press published *The Colors of Nature: Subtropical Gardens by Raymond Jungles* (2008). I can still remember the exuberance that I felt when I poured over the two dozen, mostly residential, mostly modernist, and mostly Florida-based commissions that Jungles and his collaborators realized over a period of fifteen years. Here were thoroughly original, vibrant, and exciting residential designs that were simultaneously lush, vivid, and tactile, employing mostly native subtropical plants to do the heavy lifting. The result: seductive gardens that leapt off the page.

Now, Raymond Jungles is back with a vengeance, packing another visual wallop with *The Cultivated Wild*. This latest survey of twenty-one projects picks up where *The Colors of Nature* left off. Since then, we see both a geographical expansion and a typological broadening of the firm's ambition and project work—expanding beyond Florida to such diverse locales as Big Timber, Montana; Monterrey, Mexico; St. Kitts and Nevis in the West Indies; Abacos, Bahamas; and even the temporary Brazilian Modern Orchid Show for the New York Botanical Garden in the Bronx.

This last garden, an homage to Roberto Burle Marx, reads like a response to Burle Marx's 1967 credo, *Jardim e ecologia*, in which the pioneering modernist master proclaimed, "Creating an artificial landscape does not mean denying or slavishly imitating nature. It means knowing how to transpose and knowing how to compose, on the base of a personal selection criterion, the result of a slow, intense and prolonged observation."

This design philosophy and site-specific sensitivity is present throughout this latest and more expansive survey of Jungles's work—and is enlivened, enriched, and expanded with a more diverse collection of commissions, remarkably completed during just the past decade. Here Jungles and his studio tackle a diverse array of projects including his own studio garden in Miami; public and private rooftops (e.g. the New World Symphony Rooftop Garden and the Sky Garden in Miami); botanical gardens (e.g. the Miami Beach Botanical Garden and the Brazilian Garden, Naples); a pedestrian mall (the 1100 block of Lincoln Road in Miami), hotels and private clubs (Soho Beach House Garden, Miami), and resorts/retreats (e.g. Golden Rock Inn Garden and the Pavilion Beach Club Garden, both in the West Indies).

Unlike the earlier collection of Jungles's work, which included the occasional plan and some common or Latin names of plants, this survey is profusely illustrated with general and thumbnail plans, sections, sketches, and design details that reveal the creative process. More than an ode to freehand drawing by such modernist landscape architects as Burle Marx, Garrett Eckbo, and the early residential pencil sketches of Lawrence Halprin, these "old school" hand-generated renderings allow us to understand how Jungles sees, thinks, and solves macro- and micro-scale design challenges. These highly personal, evocative plans and other supplemental drawings are rich in information that provides portals for the reader to trace how Jungles chronicles his design intent for capturing and exploiting views (not to mention the value of sky and skyline); how existing site features are protected, leveraged, and repurposed; how one may move seamlessly from inside to outside living environments (a critical modernist principle); how multipurpose spaces are crafted yielding multiple user experiences in the same space; and how a visitor experience is choreographed and manipulated from the moment of arrival.

In addition to the drawings, supplemental margin notes and narrative text capture Jungles's concern for balancing aesthetics with practicality, ease of maintenance, the visual and physical role of water, education, and interpretation (e.g. conservation, biodiversity), and, when necessary, how to design for resiliency (e.g. sea level change, withstanding weather events). Perhaps most exciting for readers with a horticultural bent, plant material decisions are made visible, capturing the thought process for the deployment of native and nonnative plants.

Finally, one theme that resonates in many of the project narratives is Jungles's quest for *harmony*. The first two projects illustrated in this survey embody this quest: the penthouse Sky Garden at 1111 Lincoln Road atop the celebrated Herzog & de Meuron–designed parking garage and the one-block pedestrian expanse along the 1100 block of Lincoln Road, which serves as its gateway while simultaneously expanding the iconic six blocks of a mall designed by Morris Lapidus in 1960. Here, along this one block-long segment of roadway turned greenway, idealized nature (inspired by the Everglades) and abstract art (the biomorphic forms of the reflecting pools) come together in a shared, symphonic, highly personal language of built and natural features that, as Jungles notes, results in "an ensemble of trees native to Florida and geometric water gardens reminiscent of the famous wetland ecosystem [that create] an inviting gathering space."

In addition to his ambition for design continuity (even at a micro scale, where "each stone was laid by hand in the tradition of Burle Marx," or as his daughter Amanda once recounted for me, that on Raymond's birthday he was in the rain, on a ladder, placing bromeliads in canopy trees), Jungles choreographs multiple venues and opportunities for spontaneous human interaction that is playfully reminiscent of Lawrence Halprin's quest to harness and leverage the kaleidoscope of life found in cities like Miami.

Lincoln Road in Miami hosts thirteen million domestic and international visitors annually, while the global art and design fairs Art Basel Miami Beach and Design Miami, held each December in Miami Beach, attract more than 70,000 visitors from around the world. Now that Jungles has leapt over the garden wall, bursting into the public realm in our streets, plazas, and botanical gardens while harnessing, as Burle Marx put it, "the genuine element of nature in all its strength and quality, as a medium organized in terms of, and for the purpose of aesthetic composition," ("Concepts of Composition in Landscape Architecture," 1954), it would appear based on this most recent survey of work that he is poised to amaze, enlighten, and nurture a broader audience with a unique design approach that he continues to refine, expand, and perfect.

This garden is the crown on the now-iconic parking garage designed by Swiss architecture firm Herzog & de Meuron that lies at the western terminus of Lincoln Road in Miami Beach. The structure has been recognized around the world for its bold and unexpected architecture, and it has quickly become one of the most visible and recognizable structures in the city.

The project, known as the Sky Garden, gave Jungles the opportunity to enhance a very unique rooftop space; a penthouse has the unusual distinction of occupying the top level of this complex, which is otherwise part parking garage, part retail space, and part event space. The overall goal was to strike a balance between aesthetic vision and practicality. The architects hung the apartment and its "front yard" from the structure's top slab, creating a sort of mezzanine space within the garage's top level. Although its high position provides it an enviable view of the city and its prominent address gives it instant distinction, the exceptionally well-designed residence is meant to be unpretentious, and to defer to the rooftop landscape for its true sense of identity.

The west side of the garden is called the Slope Garden, and is named for the way the slanted approach to the penthouse angles down gradually underneath the westernmost edge of the garage's roof; it eventually levels off 10 feet below. The Slope Garden provides an ideal vantage point for views across Biscayne Bay and toward the downtown Miami skyline. The garden was, of necessity, designed to be resilient and low maintenance. A diverse palette of native plants and noninvasive specimen plant material has adapted well to the site and to the shallow soil depths, which average 6 inches. Specimen red-trunk acacia trees from Africa provide scale and sculptural qualities while framing views toward the Atlantic Ocean in the distance. A winding zoysia grass path—left unmown to celebrate its natural mounding tendency—leads visitors through a variety of experiential moments within the space. Vines including railroad vine, Virginia creeper, and grape climb up and over the roof of the garage and the private elevator tower that extends above it, as well as hang suspended over the Slope Garden's exterior railings, giving parking patrons on the seventh-floor multiuse space below a clue about the garden's existence.

The east side of the Sky Garden has been dubbed the Entertainment Garden, and rests on the roof of the adjacent building—the former SunTrust bank, originally constructed in 1968. It includes a bar, an outdoor dining table designed by the architects, and a pool designed by Jungles. Open hardscape areas were included to accommodate large gatherings. The area formerly used as storage for the building's mechanical equipment has now become a spectacular pool framed by leaning Sabal palms, a verdant vine trellis, and an outdoor dining area—an extreme example of adaptive reuse.

The Sky Garden uses many of the same materials found on the ground-level public plaza below, known as 1111 Lincoln Road, which was also designed by Jungles. White *pedra portuguesa* stones were hand-laid and mortared on all exterior horizontal surfaces, while white river rock lines organically shaped planting beds. The garage's cast-in-place concrete slabs function as floor plates, columns, and ramps—the use of concrete and overhangs is a nod to the local vernacular. Overall, the Sky Garden's cohesive garden and hardscape design helps two very different but equally iconic structures communicate well at roof level.

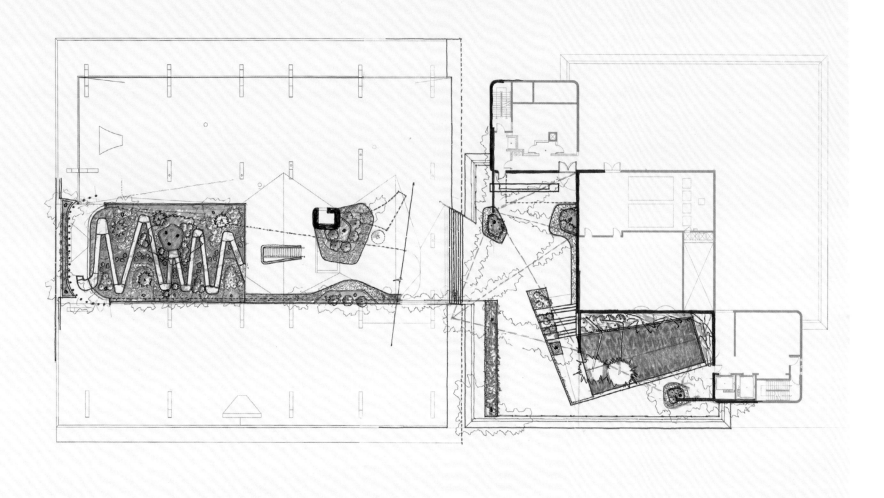

ABOVE The pool, planted steps, paving treatment, and green areas were planned in close conjunction with Christine Binswanger of Herzog & de Meuron.

OPPOSITE This section of the Sky Garden shows how it spans the Herzog & de Meuron–designed parking garage and the midcentury SunTrust building. Plants unite the two contiguous roofs into one plane of green.

PREVIOUS PAGES Plants chosen for this extraordinarily sited roof garden thrive in shallow soil and can withstand harsh winds and direct sunlight. *Ipomoea pes-caprae* and *Gaillardia pulchella*, which grow naturally on coastal sand dunes, were included, as were *Alcantarea imperialis*, *Alcantarea odorata*, and *Solandra grandiflora*.

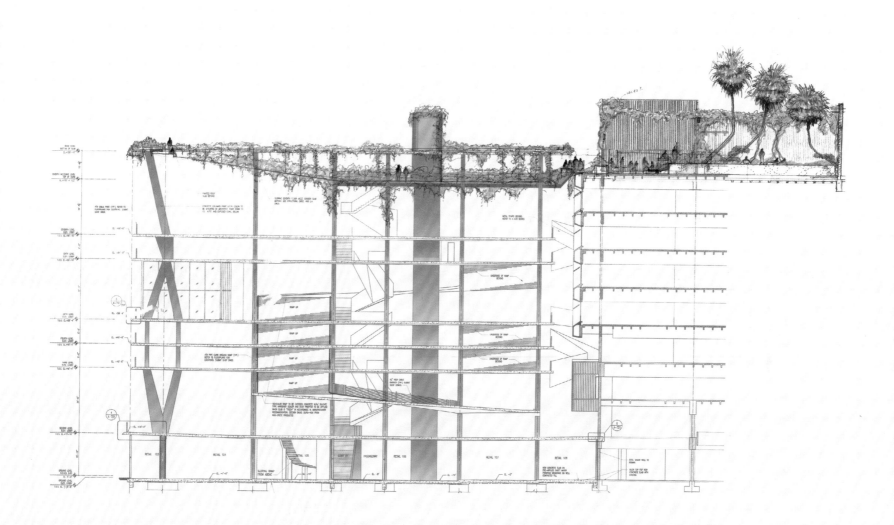

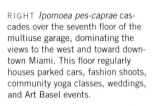

RIGHT *Ipomoea pes-caprae* cascades over the seventh floor of the multiuse garage, dominating the views to the west and toward downtown Miami. This floor regularly houses parked cars, fashion shoots, community yoga classes, weddings, and Art Basel events.

FAR RIGHT A late-afternoon view from the slope garden toward South Beach.

ABOVE Stainless-steel vine cables provide a structure for more *Ipomoea pes-caprae*, and helps it act as living architecture. This design produces ever-changing shadows on the *pedra portuguesa* pavers below.

RIGHT Tall *Sabal palmettos* add movement, drama, and scale to the facade of the SunTrust Building that fronts the rooftop pool. *Thunbergia grandiflora* 'Alba' and *Trachelospermum jasminoides*, supported by stainless-steel cables, continue the theme of abundant, suspended plant life introduced by the initial garden.

RIGHT The view from the apartment's covered loggia toward the private elevator tower that takes the owner to his parking level and then down to street level at 1111 Lincoln Road.

FAR RIGHT The view from the top of the slope garden toward the apartment. To achieve a wild-looking garden, specimen *Acacia seyal* hailing from Sítio Roberto Burle Marx are anchored in invisible planters and vines, bromeliads, agaves, and grasses grow together. The rooftop site allowed only an average soil depth of six inches.

TOP The sculptural form of an *Acacia seyal* provides drama, shade, and scale. It is surrounded by *Eragrostis elliottii*, *Muhlenbergia capillaris*, *Zoysia* spp., and seasonal wildflowers that evoke a natural meadow.

ABOVE A dense cluster of plants under the apartment's shaded terrace gives way to an open path planted with low grasses that suggests a circulation path through the slope garden.

RIGHT Herzog & de Meuron created a window to the sky above the Slope Garden and the south facade of the residence. Vigorous vines mask the Sky Garden's private elevator tower. *Agave americana* 'Gainesville Blue' and *Alcantarea imperialis* grow amid a sea of *Ipomoea pes-caprae* and *Philodendron* 'Burle Marx.'

1111 LINCOLN ROAD

This redesign for the historic promenade and plaza at 1111 Lincoln Road, developed concurrently with Herzog & de Meuron's now-iconic parking garage, completely revitalized the westernmost block of Lincoln Road Mall. Native plants and hardscape elements are carefully placed to create various vantage points and visual corridors for pedestrians—one of the project's main goals. Sight lines through the block are also preserved thanks to massings of low plants and high tree canopies to ensure that visitors can engage with retail, residential, and restaurant spaces along both sides of the street. The result is a civic space unlike any other in the city; the City of Miami Beach Planning Department's assistant director dubbed the project "the Urban Glade."

To bring nature into the center of Miami Beach along this roadway-turned-greenway, Jungles looked to the Everglades—a region with unique characteristics and a wide variety of indigenous plants—for inspiration. An ensemble of trees native to Florida and geometric water gardens reminiscent of the famous wetland ecosystem create an inviting gathering space, and turtles, fish, and the sounds of gently cascading water enliven the setting. The highly reflective pond surfaces also mirror the sky, trees, and human visitors, adding extra dimension to the narrow urban site.

Specimen cypress trees anchor the display of vegetation within the plaza; other indigenous trees also feature prominently in the design, including live oaks, pond apples, red mangroves, and Sabal palms. One nonnative tropical wetland tree was included as well—a Guiana chestnut tree. This "money tree" is indigenous to Central and South American countries. Besides tolerating shade and high water tables, it is a symbol of good fortune. It was selected for all these qualities, and was placed where other trees would falter.

The pond-maintenance equipment and mechanical systems for the entire 1100 block are contained in a sculptural vault that is melded into the design of the plaza through a series of stepped platforms. These reduce the impact of its necessary scale, which is further concealed by plants that cascade and a water element that trickles or flows slowly between the bold roots of the red mangroves. Climbing to its top level has become a local tradition for adventurous children and adults, and each stage of the ascent also provides a new vantage point over the area.

The wonderful qualities and materiality of Brazilian *pedra portuguesa* led to its use on the ground plane and throughout the project's other hardscape features. Its mosaiclike texture adds a handcrafted quality to the space and has the additional benefit of gently discouraging skateboarders. Each stone was laid by hand in the style of Roberto Burle Marx, the visionary Brazilian landscape designer. Generously proportioned concrete benches accommodate daily visitors as comfortably as small crowds viewing performances in the space. The opportunity for spontaneous human interaction now abounds in this reinvigorated area.

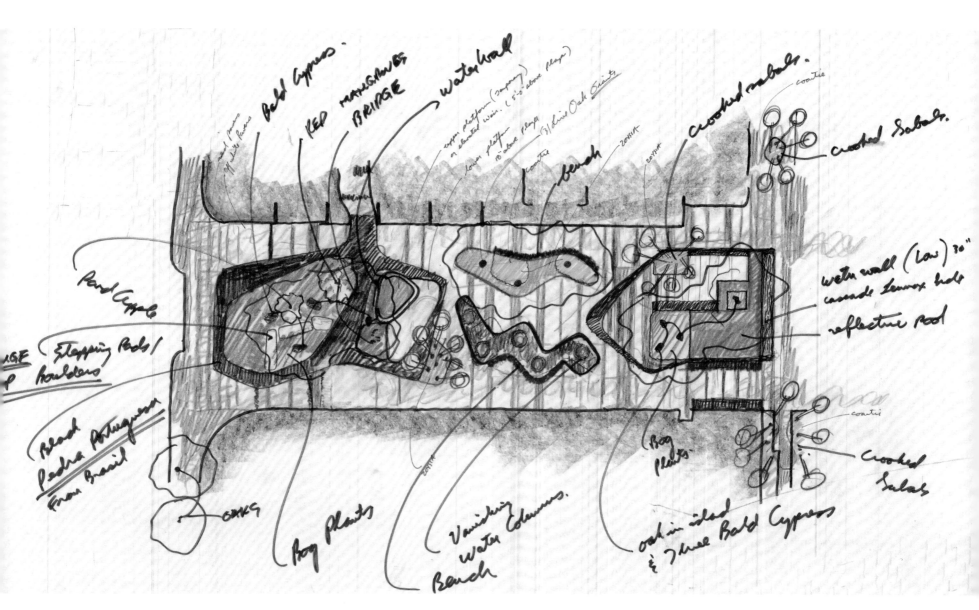

The sketch is annotated with the following handwritten labels:

- Bald Cypress
- RED MANGROVE BRIDGE
- Waterwall
- upper platform (50gpm) on elevated weir. (5'-0" above plaza)
- lower platform 18" above plaza
- (3) Live Oak Saints
- crooked sabals.
- coatie
- crooked Sabals.
- Pond Apple
- coatie
- bench
- 20 MIN
- 20 MIN
- 20 MIN
- GE (Stepping Rods / boulders
- wetn wall (Low) 30"
- cascade Lennox hole
- reflecting pool
- Black Pedra Portuguesa from Brazil
- coatie
- OAKS
- Bog Plants
- Bog Plants
- Vanishing Water Edmums. Bench
- oak in island & three Bald Cypress
- Crooked Salas

LEFT An early sketch of the plaza's sculptural vault, which conceals the mechanical equipment for all four of the water features. A series of planted platforms help to mediate the impact of its necessary scale. It has also become one of the plaza's most popular features by providing visitors "stages" for impromptu play and social interaction.

ABOVE An early sketch of the 1100 block of Lincoln Road showing different ideas for how to incorporate various programming into the long and narrow space.

PREVIOUS PAGES A view of the plaza on a typical Saturday evening. Families and friends interact beneath the canopies of *Quercus virginiana*, *Sabal palmetto*, and *Taxodium distichum*.

ABOVE The canopies of the architecture, along with the canopies of the trees, create a comfortable, shaded environment. Although restaurants line the block, outdoor seating is restricted and peripheral in order to preserve the plaza space for pedestrians.

OPPOSITE, FAR LEFT Mature *Quercus virginiana* demonstrate nature's ability to enrich a built environment by leading the eye from the plantings at ground level up to the asymmetric decks of the Herzog & de Meuron parking garage.

OPPOSITE, LEFT The plaza's westernmost water garden. The *Taxodium distichum* have flushed new leaves and the roots of a *Rhizophora mangle* anchor the plant into the water, as they would in its natural environment. These wetland plantings are part of the site's extensive biofiltration system.

LEFT, ABOVE The landscape links 40,000 square feet of retail concept stores and restaurants—all benefit commercially from the green vistas the site provides.

LEFT, BELOW Children love to explore the site's water gardens. They spot ripples made by the small fish and turtles that call this urban plaza home, or play with their own reflections.

OPPOSITE The wilds of the Everglades, mere miles to the west, are reintroduced into the city here for the public's enjoyment, earning this space the nickname "the Urban Glade."

PREVIOUS PAGES, LEFT A detail of the site's specimen *Pachira aquatica*, commonly called a money tree. An interactive glass pavilion by artist Dan Graham, behind it, reflects light from the storefronts and provides another way for visitors to engage with the site.

PREVIOUS PAGES, RIGHT A Landscape Architecture Foundation study of this site noted that 68 plant species were used in the streetscape, 90 percent of which are native to the state of Florida—10 of these native species are also endangered or threatened. Several *Sabal palmettos*, Florida's state tree, are here entwined with fragrant *Trachelospermum jasminoides*.

The primary goal for this property was to create a truly seamless indoor-outdoor living environment that could take full advantage of South Miami's light and weather. Jungles was brought in by the project's architect, Mark Hampton, to transform an outdated 1960s home with uninspired landscaping into a stylish contemporary residence with a Zen-like feel to the garden. Plays on scale and texture, a predominant design element, are created with leaf and plant forms. Color is approached artistically, with rhythm and variety providing visual pacing and interest.

Some of the only plants worth retaining were mature live oak trees and a mahogany tree near the main entry; their branches painted moving light and a playful texture on the driveway below. The clients, however, asked Jungles to create a new entry sequence because the existing, typically suburban circulation plan crowded the house and placed parking spaces in displeasingly close proximity to the front door. Jungles pushed the driveway farther away from the front entrance to gain space that would help create a sense of ceremony and arrival. Elevated asymmetric concrete platforms—pressed with rock salt for texture—now lead to a wooden deck around the trunk of the mahogany tree. The driveway itself was paved with sand to create a more soft and natural appearance, and it remains shaded by the broad canopies of the live oaks; staghorn ferns now thrive in the crooks of their lower branches, adding an established and layered effect. The clients desired ample open lawn areas in the front yard, which are afforded privacy by a dense, verdant border of native plantings along the perimeters next to adjacent lots and the street.

The existing swimming pool was in a less-than-desirable location in relation to the redesigned house, so after a series of site studies Jungles designed a new outdoor entertaining area, dining area, swimming pool, and barbecue area to link the backyard's programming with the architectural floor plan. He replaced one end of the existing swimming pool with a sculptural water element to enliven the outside dining area with soft burbles. Each distinct outdoor area presents a different view into the garden, but they are united by a meditative aura. He also dug a swimming pool in an unused part of the site, enhancing the clients' enjoyment of the full property. The redesigned swimming pool invites dips, and visually, it becomes the focal point for the most heavily used areas of the residence: the kitchen and living room. Careful thought was therefore given to what forms would reflect off the pool's surface in the daytime—and equally at nighttime, when natural moonlight and introduced lighting elements help intriguing shadows take form and fall gracefully upon the garden spaces, pool, and water element.

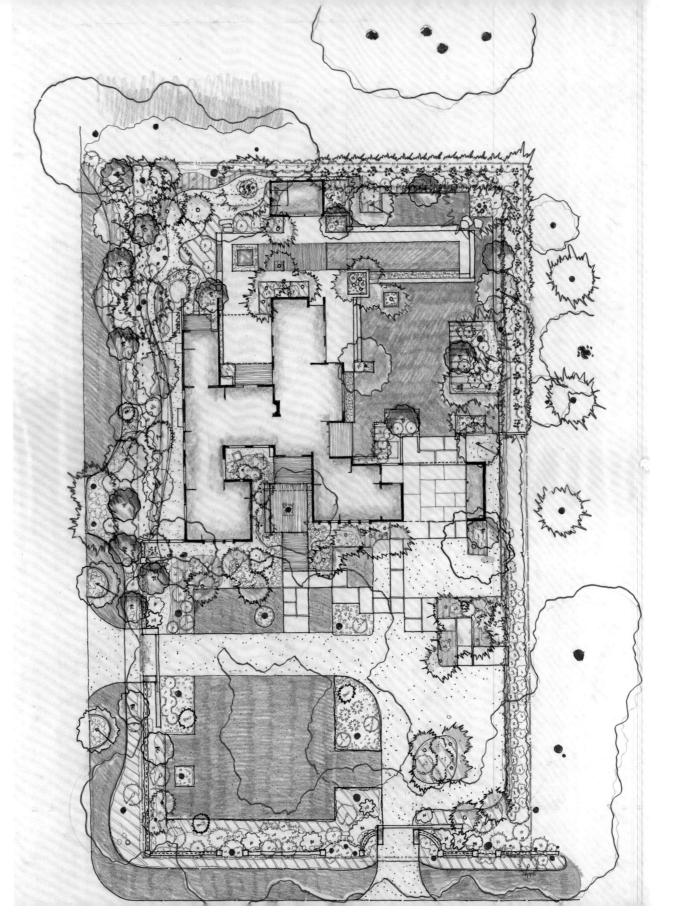

RIGHT The design development site plan. Jungles made a point of retaining the property's mature trees; their positions and canopies are outlined in blue ink.

OPPOSITE, ABOVE Existing *Quercus virginiana* trees give structure to the garden's street entrance.

OPPOSITE, BELOW Unobtrusive gravel was chosen for the driveway; it crosses the view corridor from the front door to the main garden. Low steps with straightforward geometry keep the focus on the softscape elements.

PREVIOUS PAGES A detail of the stacked-slate reflecting pool in the backyard. Water trickles evenly over its textured sides and into a rock-filled basin. This feature was introduced to enliven the view from a covered terrace between the residence's two wings.

ABOVE A healthy *Platycerium bifurcatum* is nestled in the crook of a preexisting *Quercus virginiana*, overlooking mounds of *Neomarica gracilis* and several *Aechmea* 'Dean' bromeliads. In the background, tall *Heterospathe elata* palms shelter a monocultural area of *Microsorum scolopendrium*. Pervious materials such as sand comprise 80 percent of the vehicular areas to keep the overall effect soft and natural; the balance of the paving in the street-side garden is poured-in-place concrete, scaled and textured with rock salt to give it visual interest and a rough, natural appearance.

OPPOSITE *Heliconia caribaea* 'Yellow' draws visitors into a lushly planted pathway that also includes *Philodendron* 'Burle Marx,' in the middle ground, and *Heliconia* 'Pedro Ortiz,' in the background.

LEFT Poured-in-place concrete panels in a warm tone lead from the parking area to the front entry; *Ophiopogon japonicus* 'Nana' fills the spaces between them. Palms including *Chambeyronia macrocarpa*, *Heterospathe elata*, and *Satakentia liukiuensis* mediate the scale of the existing architecture.

ABOVE Curved *Heterospathe elata* palms look like they have been growing in the yard for years, but were added specifically to lean into the open space above one end of the pool deck.

ABOVE A stacked-stone water wall edges one side of the pool, providing pleasant sounds and drama when illuminated at night and adding visual interest to the feature as viewed from inside the residence.

RIGHT A travertine-and-îpe-wood wall floats in front of what appears to be the edge of a dense jungle, ordering the verdant space with its clean lines and sculptural form.

This garden began as an imaginative study in what could survive the toughest of beachfront conditions. The client, Bob Davids, is an entrepreneur known for creating successful businesses as varied as a winery and a toy company. He purchased a simple, demure 1960s beach house and two small lots that total half an acre in 1994. The house was destroyed by Hurricane Floyd in September 1999, and the entire site was left to "dry out" until 2001. A remodel began in 2002 with a view to creating a house and garden that could withstand future storms; all of the garden spaces lie less than 20 feet from the mean high water line, which proved to be the biggest design challenge. Davids, who comes from a construction family, acted as general contractor.

The design quickly evolved to focus on creating interesting and durable textures. To that end, the hardscape and landscape palette is primarily composed of local materials and indigenous species. The swimming pool and garden have minimal maintenance requirements and can withstand the elements: harsh sun, salt spray, and occasional gale-force sea breezes. Plant species that have low water needs and that are appropriate to the site figure prominently. Indigenous plants provide habitat for local birds and insects, and a few accent plants and coconut palms are mixed in for visual interest.

Davids lived in Asia for thirteen years and wanted to imbue the project with the "tropical-colonial" mood he often encountered in his travels. The new house was therefore based on a "butterfly" concept, meaning that each room in the interior is somehow mirrored on the exterior. The resulting floor plan places much of the house's 4,200 square feet of living space in direct communication with the garden. This gave Jungles even more impetus—and latitude—to create outdoor environments for entertaining and outdoor living.

Jungles utilized the entire site and borrowed the beachfront landscape's vistas to create a deeply immersive visual and auditory dialogue between the visitor and the garden. Water is an important recurring motif in this scheme, and water elements in particular create drama for visitors approaching the residence. As they enter the garden from a heavily planted roadway that provides a privacy buffer, they pass along a boardwalk that meanders through and over four water features including a series of waterfalls and streams that pass through—and reflect—sculpted rock formations. Bridges connected by an old nautical rope Davids discovered during a fishing excursion lead pedestrians naturally to the front doors.

Water also links the landscape to the sea lavender–draped shoreline beyond as it spills over the edge of an infinity pool and echoes the lapping of the tide. In a reversal of usual designs that place a pool's infinity edge out toward a horizon or view, here it faces in toward the garden; this animates the space and creates the optical illusion that the pool is the source of the water for the streams that run through the property. The pool sits as close to the beach as possible, with a swim-out area complete with spa jets.

ABOVE To guard against occasional but fiercely strong storms, an erosion-control fence was installed and the beach was planted with *Argusia gnaphalodes*, *Gaillardia pulchella*, *Hymenocallis latifolia*, *Ipomoea pes-caprae*, *Suriana maritima*, and *Uniola paniculata*. These add texture and color—as well as stability—to the waterfront property.

OPPOSITE The site plan shows how close the house lies to the beach; plantings perform the crucial function of shielding it from the high water line.

PREVIOUS PAGES The pool's water mimics the hue of the ocean, helping the feature to engage with the horizon line. The mid-pool planter at left is home to a specimen *Latania*, *Aechmea* 'Dean' bromeliads, and a *Portulaca afra*. The stone is indigenous limestone.

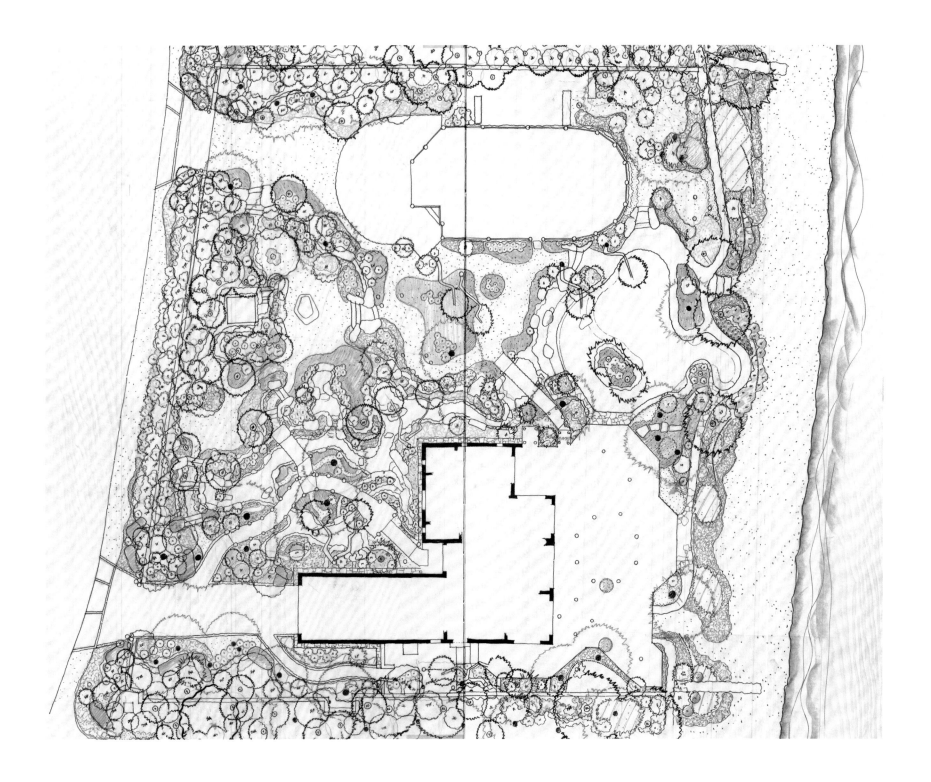

CLOCKWISE FROM TOP LEFT A casual garden path of crushed shell is lined by colorful plants including *Portea* 'Jungles' and *Microsorum scolopendrium*. One of four separate water cascades that provide a "stereo" sound of natural noises—a client request. *Argusia gnaphalodes*, also known as sea lavender, is an indigenous plant with a soft texture that thrives on the beachfront. A shallow lounging area is fitted with a Balinese stone table and stools; the pool's infinity edge spills landward, into the garden spaces, creating a peaceful envelope of sound.

OPPOSITE The pool garden lies so close to the water that it appears to be a natural extension of the ocean.

ABOVE The pool garden as seen from the terrace of a two-story thatch guest hut. Palms on the site are a mix of *Coccothrinax* sp., *Cocos nucifera*, and *Sabal domingensis*.

RIGHT At sunset colors fuse, linking the garden to the ocean beyond.

This specialty garden encompasses one acre within the larger Naples Botanical Garden. The goal behind its creation was to bring a bold and distinctively Brazilian garden to the public, one designed specifically to celebrate the late Roberto Burle Marx's prodigious and inventive legacy, humanistic spirit, and love of plants. It contains lawn and plaza areas that provide venues for diverse cultural events such as watercolor workshops, jazz concerts, yoga classes, and movie screenings—and allows them to take place without disturbing other visitors to the larger garden. Its design encourages visitors to interact with the garden by smelling and touching the flora, and the resulting interplay between people and plants creates a convivial setting for garden enthusiasts and botanists alike.

Educating visitors about Brazil's incredible biodiversity was one of Jungles's goals. He immersed himself in research about Brazilian plants and found the process of learning more about them a welcome challenge. Brazil's seven individual terrestrial ecosystems are represented in successive plantings along an accessible poured-concrete walkway, and each plant is displayed as if it were in its natural habitat to help it achieve its greatest potential for growth. Viewed here, amid the restored natural wetlands of Naples, Florida, these create both an aesthetic and a cultural dialogue. Emphasis was also placed on educating the public about conservation of Brazil's natural resources—many of its natural systems are sources of great mystery to U.S. audiences. Each of these ecosystems features plants with one or more particularly unique attributes, such as an unusual color, form, texture, fragrance, or medicinal use.

The Brazilian Garden's focal point, a vibrant elevated water garden plaza, uses scale to create a distinctive public space. Set against the backdrop of a restored conservation area, the plaza features an 8-by-17-foot Roberto Burle Marx ceramic tile mural donated by Jungles—his only public mural in the United States. The mural is the focal point and terminus of the programmed view and circulation plan that leads out from a visitor center. Florida's blue sky reflects off the placid black water of the upper water garden, which flows around massive *Victoria amazonica* water lilies that resemble floating stepping stones and eventually tumbles down an infinity-edged, multitiered cascading waterfall into a lower pond. Brazilian palms and specimen trees add sculptural, cultural, and visual meaning to the garden; Burle Marx personally discovered many of these species on his excursions in the Brazilian wilderness or propagated them at his nursery in Barra de Guaratiba, near Rio. Other native Brazilian plants such as water plants, epiphytes, vines, and orchids are featured throughout the garden.

The overall design of the Brazilian Garden was inspired as much by Raymond's knowledge of Brazilian flora as by his artistic interpretation of the site. As the sun sets behind the plaza's vine trellis, the hues of the sky mimic the hues of Burle Marx's mosaic. As dusk descends and the garden's visual elements drift away into darkness, the auditory elements created by the waterfalls take over as the garden's most prominent source of sensory stimulus, providing an unexpected and deeply soothing nighttime experience.

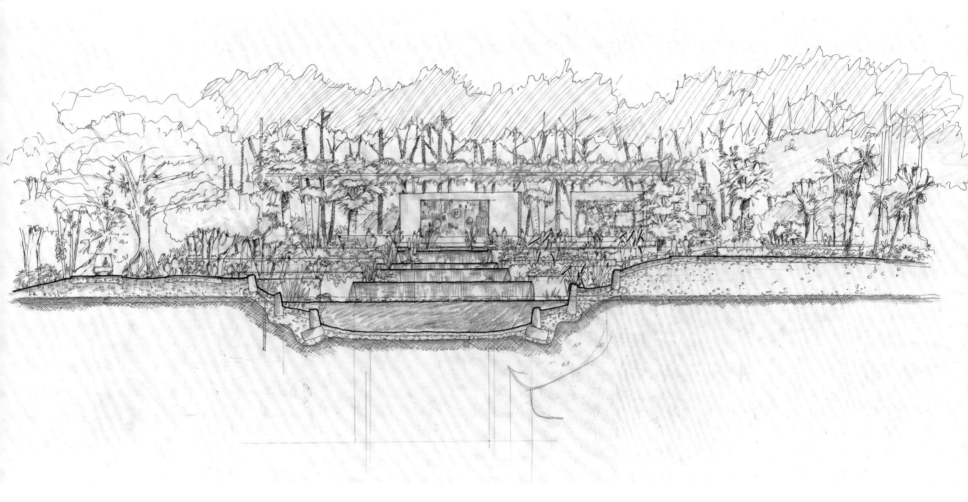

ABOVE An early hand-drawn section of the garden showing an idea for the waterfall, the placement of the Burle Marx mural, and a stone retaining wall.

RIGHT Jungles's layered planting plan, showing handwritten plant names. All plant species are Brazilian and are loosely organized to represent the various ecosystems in Brazil. Plants were laid out on site by Jungles with assistance from the Naples Botanical Garden horticultural staff.

PREVIOUS PAGES In warmer months, the Burle Marx plaza's water surface is covered by four-to-six-foot *Victoria* x 'Longwood Hybrid' water lilies. Perimeter plantings include *Acrocomia aculeata, Aechmea blanchetiana* 'Orange Form,' *Alcantarea imperialis*, and *Butia eriospatha*.

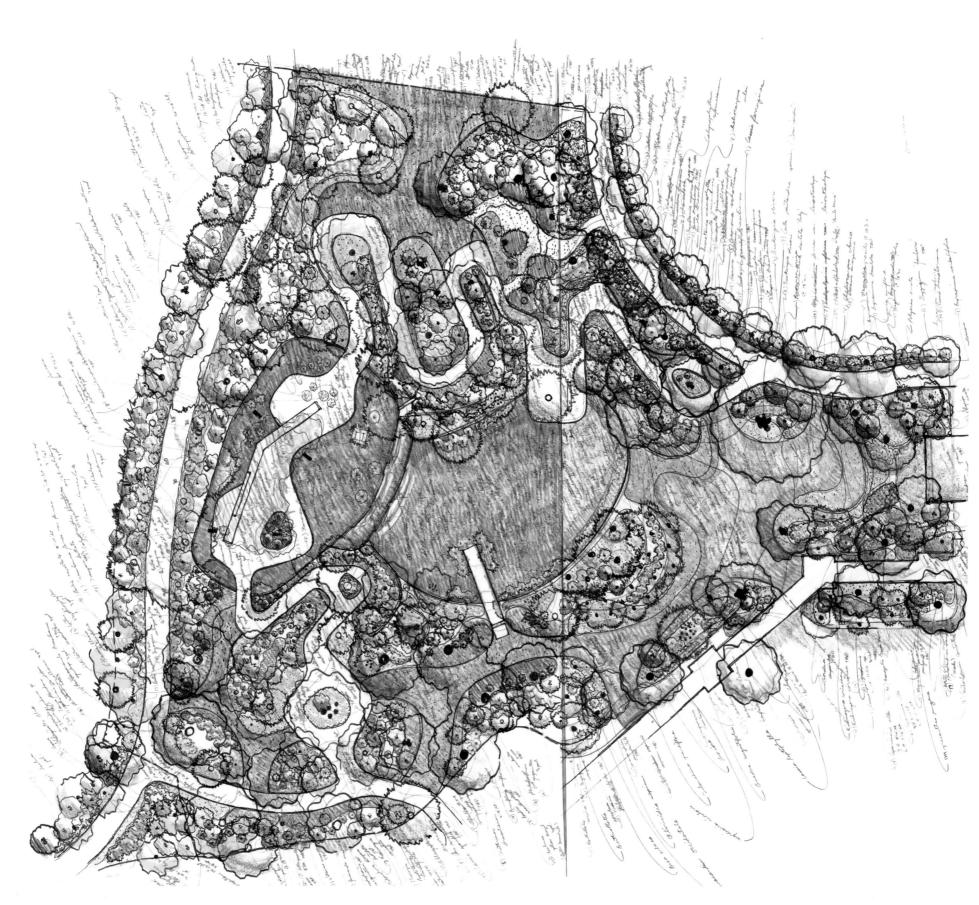

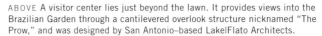

ABOVE A visitor center lies just beyond the lawn. It provides views into the Brazilian Garden through a cantilevered overlook structure nicknamed "The Prow," and was designed by San Antonio–based LakelFlato Architects.

RIGHT A concrete plank that juts into the lower water garden's pool brings visitors close to the cascades and plants, which include *Chloroleucon tortum*, *Combretum fruticosum*, and *Pitcairnia angustifolia*, which is found draped over the concrete retaining walls. *Pinus elliottii* tower beyond the mural, in the conservation area. Vines have been planted at the base of the cable-and-stainless-steel-mesh arbor, and will eventually shade the plaza.

PREVIOUS PAGES A glimpse of the Roberto Burle Marx mural donated by Jungles, seen through the trunks of *Copernicia prunifera* palms that are planted amid bromeliad species *Portea* 'Jungles.'

ABOVE Concrete weirs of various elevations and lengths reduce the visual mass of the walls and create variation in the splashing waterfall sounds. Cost-effective exposed concrete was used for all hardscape elements, a design decision strongly influenced by Burle Marx's Fazenda Vargem Grande in São Paulo, Brazil.

RIGHT Water circulates from an adjacent lake, through the Brazilian Garden, and then back into the lake.

FAR RIGHT The terraced water garden was designed with concealed safety features that do not detract from the waterfall's drama.

RIGHT, ABOVE Meandering poured-concrete walkways with a maximum slope of 1:20, for accessibility, lead visitors through a tour of planted areas that represent Brazil's seven ecosystems. Here Florida's dramatic sunlight illuminates *Alcantarea odorata*, *Myrciaria cauliflora*, and *Neoregelia* 'Jill.'

RIGHT, BELOW AND FAR RIGHT *Victoria* x 'Longwood Hybrid' water lilies float gently in the upper plaza's water garden. The pond is shallow next to pedestrian paths, but four feet deep at the weir. The lilies are planted in deeper, recessed planters.

NEW WORLD SYMPHONY ROOFTOP GARDEN

Miami Beach, Florida | 2011

Gehry Partners first contacted Jungles during the initial design phase for the New World Symphony building, which has become an icon of Miami Beach architecture. A kickoff meeting in Los Angeles in 2006 commenced with a fruitful exchange of drawings that helped to generate ideas for its eventual 7,950-square-foot rooftop space. Jungles was also selected to design planting plans for nearby streetscapes that would link the actual performance hall to its campus expansion, located just blocks from the bustle of Lincoln Road and the beach.

After seeing the preliminary models for the campus grounds during the conceptual charette, Jungles was prompted to design with shade in mind. It was clear to him that all of the peripheral areas between the hall and Lincoln Road, the convention center, and around the site itself would benefit from cooling shade. Jungles designed streetscapes and selected specimen live oaks—chosen for their longevity and broad, leafy canopies—to add verdure along the vehicular passages. The streets surrounding the campus are now lined with trees on both sides, creating corridors that suggest rhythm and movement. He also brought a touch of unexpectedly welcome informality into the urban core by using trees that are multi-stemmed and leaving them to grow unchecked. This type of environment is conducive to both relaxation and habitat creation. Simple, clean hardscape elements flow seamlessly throughout the entire campus and unify it visually.

The initial emphasis on the rooftop design was to refine its functionality and space, and Jungles worked with Gehry Partners' Craig Webb on numerous quick schemes that would provide shade and seating. Through these studies the design, which had originally focused on hardscape elements, a trellis, and flowering vines, shifted to emphasize more substantial plantings. The final planters are allotted ample space on the rooftop, and were designed to carry the load of mature gumbo limbos and specimen *Clusia rosea* trees.

The distinctive architecture of the symphony hall itself inspires its fellows to explore and create music, while the rooftop landscape provides shade and creates opportunities for outdoor education, impromptu musical performances, and receptions. Many visitors have remarked on how, upon entering its six-story-high atrium, one of the first things they notice is the dappled light created by the canopies of shade trees planted high above that filters down through an immense skylight.

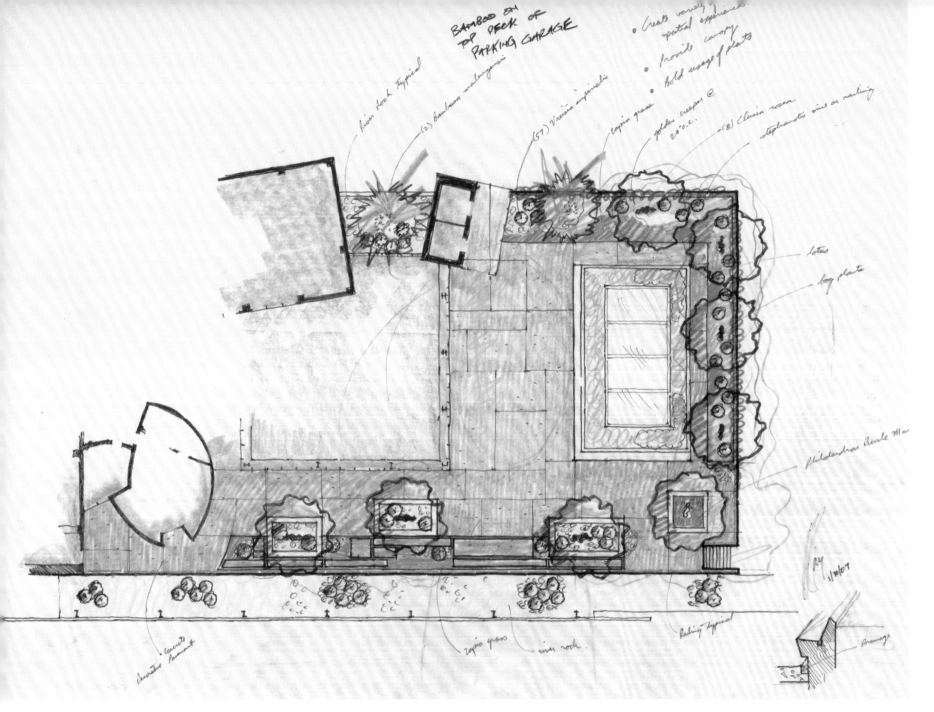

BAMBOO ON
TOP DECK OF
PARKING GARAGE

• Create variety of
  spatial experiences
• Provide canopy
• Bold usage of plants

River Rock Typical

(2) Bambusa multiplex

(57) Vireya anpionida

Zoysia grass

golden creeper @
24" o.c.

(8) Clusia rosea

stephanotis vine on railing

lotus

bog plants

Philodendron Burle Marx

Zoysia grass

river rock

Decorative Concrete Pavement

Railing Typical

Drainage

ABOVE An early revised concept sketch. Jungles worked closely with Craig
Webb of Gehry Partners to ensure the rooftop would accommodate planters of
a sufficient depth to support mature shade trees.

OPPOSITE The eastern facade of the New World Symphony. Artwork and live
concert feeds are often projected onto the building for the public's enjoyment.

PREVIOUS PAGES The rooftop garden hosts music students, symphony patrons, and events and receptions. Native *Bursera simaruba* trees and *Tripsacum
dactyloides* grasses connect the roof with the broader environment.

ABOVE Jungles designed shared seating areas and positioned them to offer clear views to the Atlantic Ocean.

RIGHT Open spaces on the terrace are designed to accommodate crowds during receptions. The concrete benches support the symphony's fundraising efforts by offering naming opportunities. *Acacia seyal* and *Clusia rosea* trees offer shade while *Muhlenbergia capillaris* grasses provide texture and color.

ABOVE The view from the elevator arrival reveals the prominent trunk of an *Acacia seyal*. Flowering *Muhlenbergia capillaris* and specimen *Clusia rosea* trees fill and surround an elevated planter with a skylight in the center that floods the auditorium many stories below.

RIGHT *Philodendron* 'Burle Marx,' from Sítio Burle Marx, thrives on the rooftop.

FAR RIGHT *Bursera simaruba* trees, selected for their resilience even in hurricane-force winds, are underplanted with large *Alcantarea imperialis* and *Ernodea littoralis* groundcover, which produces delicate pink flowers.

If these clients had their druthers they would be living in a tree house, so Jungles's task was to assist them as they renovated an uninspired 1957 structure, which had good bones, until the architecture allowed for the interior to seamlessly meld with the outdoors and views were directed onto greenery. The owners have a young son, a dachshund named Bonzai, a love of natural materials, and an abundance of Brazilian furniture. Their priorities were comfortable seating areas and an environment that would encourage quiet contemplation.

The 14,240-square-foot corner lot is located on an island dredged from surrounding Biscayne Bay by Carl Fisher, one of Miami's pioneering developers, in 1924. As the lead on the design team, Jungles was able to maximize the possibilities for creating harmony between interior and exterior spaces. He designed all of the exterior architectural elements, selected the house's windows and doors, and worked closely with the in-house architect of the general contractor to ensure interior spaces would communicate well with the open air. An architectural consultant and interior designer were brought on at a later date to refine and finalize unresolved details.

The property's most notable architectural intervention is introduced in the entry garden, which lies between two auto courts. A high-design pergola, floating concrete steps, aquatic sculpture garden, and pivoting front door create visual comfort and simultaneous sensory stimulation for those arriving and departing. As the door opens, interior and exterior elements fuse and long views both through the house and out into the garden are revealed. The same materials are used on the house's ground plane, walls, and ceiling as on the exterior, further linking the spaces.

Long walls of windows connect the primary exterior spaces with the interior, allowing in both views and light. Corner windows were introduced to magnify these opportunities; conversely, the glazing is frosted above exterior equipment areas where no view is desired. A favorite garden room with modern louvers was expanded so that it now opens up to the surrounding private courtyard garden. The remodeled kitchen functions as the center of the home's social spaces, and an outdoor dining area with a built-in table and cooktop was created adjacent to it to encourage outdoor dining and a union with nature.

Jungles uses indigenous plants to create privacy, specifically choosing species that will continue to grow larger canopies or fill in abundantly over time. These include gumbo limbo, Jamaican caper, marlberry, silver saw palmetto, golden creeper, and coontie. The existing rear garden was mostly taken up by a swimming pool, a walled-off equipment area, and pavement—a stagnant space with nondescript detailing. The scale of the swimming pool was reduced to make room for a wet deck/alternate patio perfect for lounging. This results in multiple user experiences in the same space, and also affords a long view across the garden and up to classic royal palms whose fronds wave against the skyline.

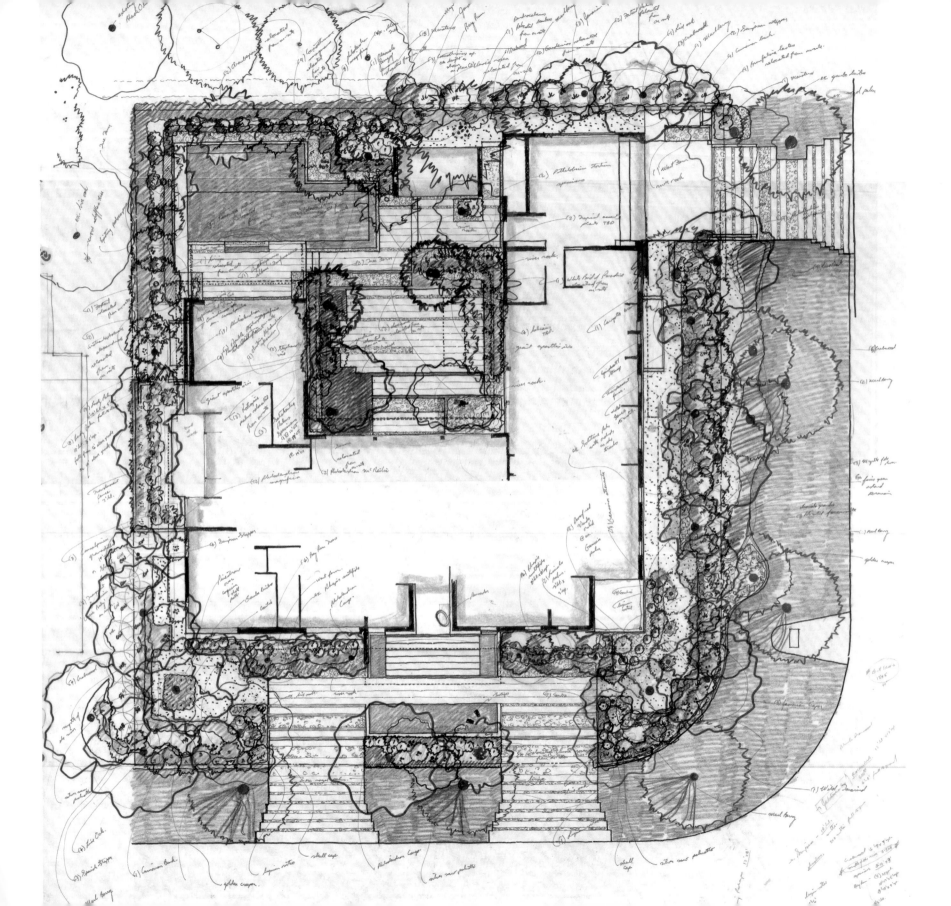

ABOVE The entry corridor's vertical and horizontal finishes provide an effective foil to the view of abundant plant life just outside.

OPPOSITE The final site plan, showing Jungles's handwritten plant identifications.

PREVIOUS PAGES Water cascades beneath the entry steps and into a water garden that replaced a typical suburban circular driveway. Jungles designed the exterior architecture elements as well as the garden, and selected the sculpture, *Testigos*, by Colombian artist Hugo Zapata.

FAR LEFT Jungles created garden "portals" that fuse inside spaces with exterior spaces. Dense plantings buffer the property from streets immediately adjacent.

LEFT, ABOVE Jungles positioned all of the house's windows and doors to maximize and frame positive views and minimize negative views.

LEFT, BELOW The view from the master bedroom looks out onto a broad terrace and the pool. The pergola extends the living space and integrates it with the garden while sliding screens offer privacy. A linear stone trough floats above the pool's water cascade and conceals a fire element. Relocated low *Coccothrinax miraguama* trees add texture at eye level.

LEFT, ABOVE A detail of a *Platycerium bifurcatum* epiphyte.

LEFT A detail of a *Nymphaea* 'Blue Beauty' from the entry water garden.

RIGHT The branches of a specimen *Myrcianthes fragrans* tree cast shadows onto the master bedroom's privacy screen and terrace. The pool's spillover edge is concealed by a narrow border of river rocks.

ABOVE The outdoor dining area features a custom concrete table with an integrated cooktop. Plantings include *Chloroleucon tortum*, a *Myrcianthes fragrans* draped in *Tillandsia usneoides*, *Philodendron* 'Rojo Congo,' and the broad-leaved *Anthurium faustomirandae*.

RIGHT The same palette of hardscape materials was used wherever possible in the vehicular areas, on the interior, and in the pool garden to provide the smallish lot with visual continuity.

OPPOSITE Jungles selected the windows and designed all visible exterior architectural elements and much of the interior architecture—all with the aim of enhancing the property's relationship to the gardens.

The Miami Beach Botanical Garden, created in 1962 as a city park, is a 2.6-acre green space in the heart of the city that makes up in tremendous diversity of plant life what it lacks in size. The garden recently benefited from a $1.2 million landscape renovation funded and managed by a public-private partnership with the Miami Beach Garden Conservancy and the City of Miami Beach. With the constraints of this somewhat limited budget, Jungles and his team decided to make the most of what was already there. In designing the overall site's hardscape and softscape elements, they chose to change the elements of the existing garden that would have the most impact and to create a variety of garden rooms that would each have its own character and energy. The design is ultimately about an articulation of spaces: gathering spaces, spaces for contemplation, intimate spaces, and public spaces.

A new, processional entry unfolds gradually as visitors move into the garden. Jungles created a very long sight line from the main gate, which seems to magnify the scale of the elements that are immediately visible. Water is a vital element in the overall scheme. Water plants in general are a tremendous way to add botanical diversity; their pond-based habitat also means that essential open space is retained and the surface can reflect the taller plant life around it, in effect doubling the amount of vegetation registered by the eye. A large water garden at the center of the space here welcomes the sky into the botanical garden, animates the space, and enlivens the landscape. On a practical level, water also aids in cooling the areas directly around the buildings.

Native plants, once only tucked into a designated corner of the garden and treated as a novelty, are now distributed throughout, and their performance in the urban environment is highlighted. Large quantities of these are layered to weave together the urban habitat; they also attract and provide refuge for insects, birds, and other creatures, which in turn enrich and enliven the space. The garden's house horticulturalist gave Jungles a "wish list" of plants to incorporate into his design; Jungles added as many as possible, and the final plant palette includes flowering trees, palms, cycads, and other subtropical plants with a scale suitable to the garden's available space.

Jungles and his team also suggested upgrades to the existing buildings to promote increased circulation. In order to accommodate this change, the garden's existing nursery and propagation areas were relocated to the northeast corner of the garden. These design interventions—performed for both artistic and practical reasons—allow the garden to schedule simultaneous events on the grand lawn and exterior terraces, and have subsequently increased the garden's rental appeal and overall capacity. Social gatherings include the garden's annual outdoor "Taste of the Garden," a weekly green market, garden yoga, theatrical performances, and private wedding receptions. Free general admission makes the garden a valuable resource for locals seeking respite from the congestion of Miami Beach and a destination for plant-minded tourists.

ABOVE Jungles dedicated a large portion of the property, outside the entry gates, to becoming a shaded public plaza. The function determined form and scale.

OPPOSITE An early site plan for the relatively diminutive botanical garden. Garden circulation and paved areas were revealed in conjunction with the garden's plant collection, both existing and proposed.

PREVIOUS PAGES An underwhelming original brick fountain was reimagined with an indigenous oolite veneer. *Thrinax radiata* palms surround it and frame views to the larger water garden beyond.

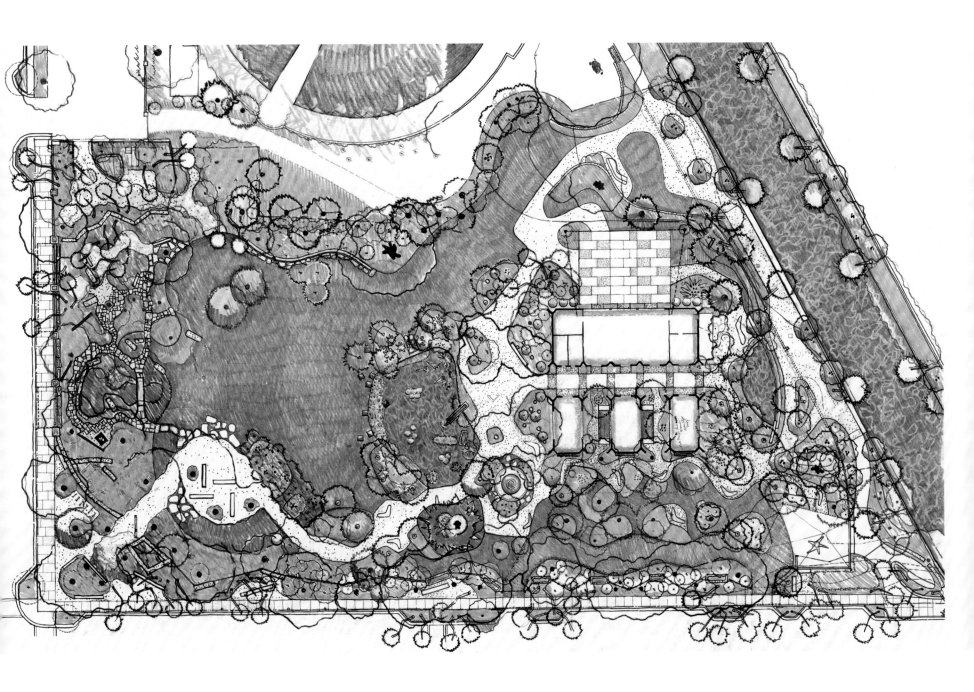

LEFT Wildflowers and grasses envelop the water garden.

BELOW A monolith of oolite stone was carved into a fountain; it floats over the pond and gently spills water into it, creating movement and sound.

OPPOSITE The view toward the Great Lawn, which is used for civic events. Many existing palms were relocated and grouped to give them a stronger collective presence.

PREVIOUS PAGES The garden offers a peaceful respite from the surrounding urban environment, which is dominated by concrete. Plantings include *Bursera simaruba*, *Copernicia macroglossa*, *Cyperus alternifolius*, *Ernodea littoralis*, *Guaiacum sanctum*, *Monstera deliciosa*, *Salvia leucantha*, and *Taxodium distichum*. An iconic curving *Sabal palmetto* anchors the space.

OVERLEAF, LEFT A detail of an area that includes *Agave angustifolia*, *Ruellia brittoniana*, and the mottled trunk of a *Copernicia fallaensis*.

OVERLEAF, RIGHT Light filters through the thorny branches of a *Chloroleucon tortum* and onto the architectural leaves of a *Copernicia macroglossa* and a blooming *Portea* 'Jungles.'

ELOISE PAVILION ROOFTOP GARDEN

Miami Beach, Florida | 2013

This one-of-a-kind South Beach rooftop garden was named after the client's loving dog, Eloise. Originally, the outdoor space surrounding this 3,000-square-foot, two-bedroom, two-and-a-half-bath penthouse featured a two-level roof deck with a poor circulation plan that limited access and usage. Jungles corrected this dilemma and eliminated some of the space's complexity simply by repositioning the garden's entrance. One sadly unusable space that wasted an enviable view has now become three functional outdoor "rooms" with the capacity for shared or private programming, and is an asset that attracts renters when the client is away.

One of Jungles's first moves was to remove a dated-looking and partially above-ground hot tub and to design a swimming pool with an internal hot tub that lies flush with the surrounding deck. The pool extends all the way to the edge of the building, giving guests the impression they could swim right out into the ocean beyond. It is the space's most prominent feature, especially at night when fiber-optic filaments embedded in its tiles sparkle like constellations. It is sized to invite lounging and gazing out at the large container ships awaiting entrance to the Port of Miami.

There was virtually no vegetation on the original rooftop, merely a sea of red mulch. Jungles placed great emphasis on keeping all views out to the horizon unobstructed; to that end, plantings around the perimeter feature low-growing plants or those that drape over planter walls. Conversely, taller silver buttonwood and bay cedar trees strategically mask the overbearing presence of neighboring residential towers. Railroad vine, which blankets native dunes, climbs vertically on the building's facade to visually connect the space to the beachfront below as well as to screen unavoidable mechanical equipment. Predominantly native species that can thrive in extremely windy conditions and that can cope with aggressive salt sprays and direct sunlight on a daily basis form the space's plant palette.

The overall aesthetic for the finish materials was greatly influenced by the client's love of sailing. Details such as îpe-wood decking and pool coping, glossy white planters, and built-in wall seats are meant to evoke the feeling of being on a boat. With informality and flexibility in mind, Jungles designed a furniture layout plan that leaves programming for the rooftop spaces undefined. The deck can easily be prepared as a setting for an intimate dinner or cleared to make room for sunbathing and yoga.

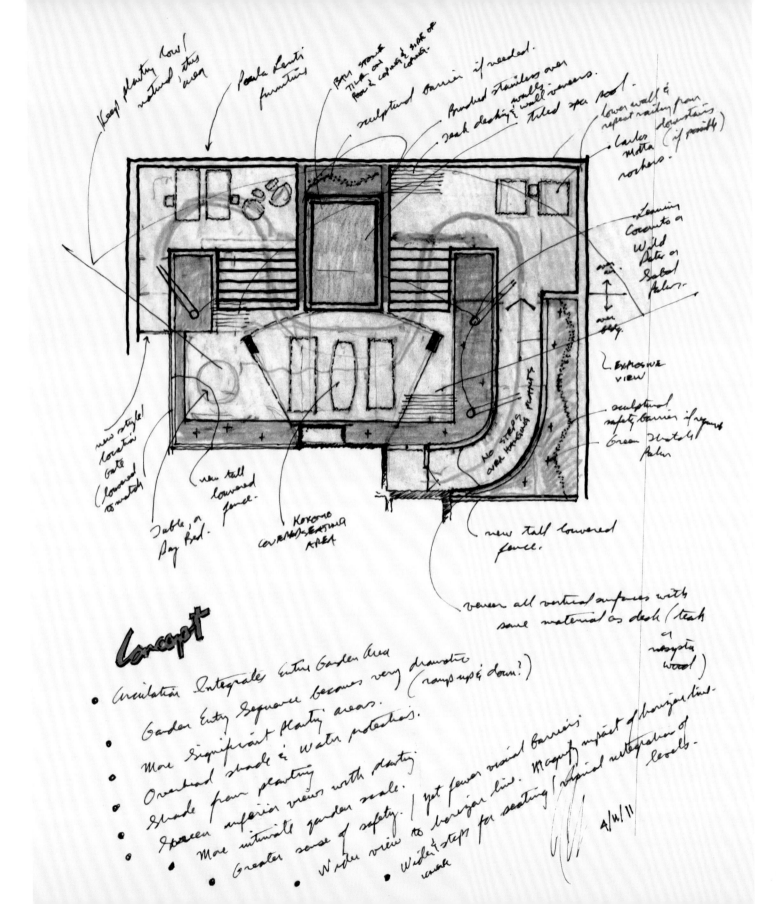

Concept

- Circulation Integrates Entire Garden Area
- Garden Entry Sequence becomes very dramatic. (ramps up & down?)
- More Significant Planting areas.
- Overhead shade & Water protection.
- Shade from planting
- Screen superior views with planting
- More intimate garden scale.
- Greater sense of safety. / yet fewer visual barriers.
- Wider view to horizon line. Magnify impact of horizon line.
- Wider & steps for seating / Vertical integration of levels.

4/14/11

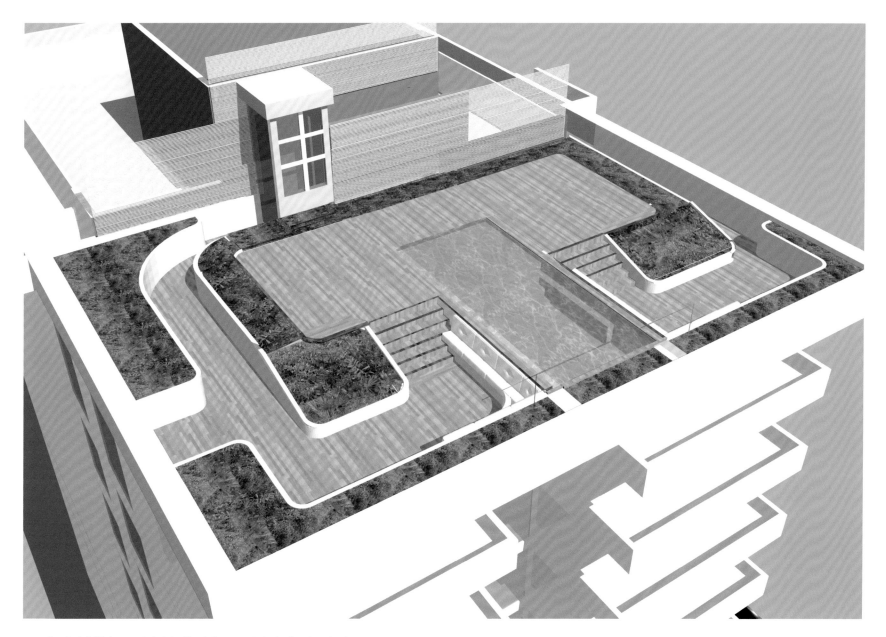

LEFT Jungles's initial concept sketch. Circulation was strategically reimagined to engage previously unused areas of the penthouse garden space.

ABOVE A design development study. A spa was added in the shallow area of the larger pool, which was extended to the edge of the roof. The overall design features emulate the characteristics of a particular yacht the owner admires.

PREVIOUS PAGES The garden overlooks South Beach and South Pointe Park Pier, which the pool was designed to blend into, visually.

RIGHT The garden sustains constant harsh wind, sun, and salt spray, so resilient plants were selected including *Portulaca oleracea* 'Puerto Rico Purple,' *Sesuvium portulacastrum*, and *Suriana maritima*.

OPPOSITE, ABOVE A detail of *Argusia gnaphalodes* and *Portulaca oleracea* 'Puerto Rico Purple.'

OPPOSITE, BELOW The îpe-wood deck and pool coping gives the garden a nautical feel. The lower deck, once isolated, is now an integral part of the entry procession.

ABOVE The garden entry corridor. Reflective white planters and recessed lighting evoke being on a yacht adrift at sea.

RIGHT Fiber-optic lighting links the pool with the stars on clear nights; the feature unites the garden with the sea and the sky simultaneously.

COCONUT GROVE GARDEN

Coconut Grove, Florida | 2010

The owners of a family compound that includes architecture of different styles and scales looked to landscape design to meld the disparate buildings together, and to meld the whole property seamlessly with its surroundings. This exceptional 3.35-acre site is located on the Miami Rock Ridge, which varies from 4 to 20 feet in elevation and consists of outcroppings of prehistoric oolitic marine limestone that range in age from 12,000 to 26 million years old. Jungles's design reinterprets how preservation efforts can be approached and reveals how a site's constraints can yield creative solutions. The completed garden space effectively returns the animated site to its ecological and subtropical origins.

When Jungles first approached the site, it held two particularly interesting extant features: an eighty-year-old East Indian Banyan tree that crowned the ridge and straddled three different residential lots, and a historic residence that had once been home to both William Jennings Bryan and Robert Frost. During the course of a six-year development, eleven additional properties were annexed and four residential structures were removed to create space for expansive gardens. The design evolved as each new piece of land was acquired. When the buildings that once crowded the magnificent specimen Banyan tree were removed, Jungles noticed, the tree flourished.

A continuous design language based on a site-specific use of materials, indigenous plantings, and water elements now visually unites the diverse property. Monolithic slabs of the oolitic limestone play a key role in organizing the site for pedestrian circulation, strengthening its connections to the residential structures, and articulating boundaries where it is used to create landforms and sculptural outdoor spaces. Eighty percent of the stone was excavated on site, in alignment with the project's ecological goals. For a long time, the site looked less like a residential area than a dust-filled quarry filled with excavators; in reality, the workmen were carefully carving out blocks that Jungles had marked with fluorescent lines from his spray paint wand—his on-site pencil.

Habitat was gradually reestablished. Trees once common to the now-vanishing tropical hardwood hammock were planted, including live oak, milkbark, gumbo limbo, lignum vitae, and pigeon plum. More than five hundred palms, cycads, and fragrant flowering trees and shrubs were brought in to enhance the final space and to imbue it with a provocative variety.

The natural oolite formations inspired Jungles to design two grottos for the property. The first acts as a transition space between two houses of different architectural styles while creating privacy for both. In 2004, a hurricane uprooted a nearby oak tree, but Jungles saw it as an opportunity to reposition it so that its sprawling branches could lean evocatively over the grotto. Water trickles into the area from a carved oolite fountain basin, staining the stone with a desirable patina of calcium deposits and moss. The whole scene is framed by foliage with contrasting shapes and textures, including *Philodendron wilsonii* and silver saw palmetto. The limestone excavated from one house's basement was reused to build a second grotto, which was designed primarily to capture storm water and to prevent it from entering the same building again.

Oolite excavated from the property was reused to build a lagoon along its lower ridge. The lagoon is dug 13 feet below the water table, so it is filled directly by groundwater, which rises and falls rhythmically with the tide. Sabal palms with plenty of character fringe these green-stained, 20-foot-high stone monoliths that line the lagoon and mask its large pump house.

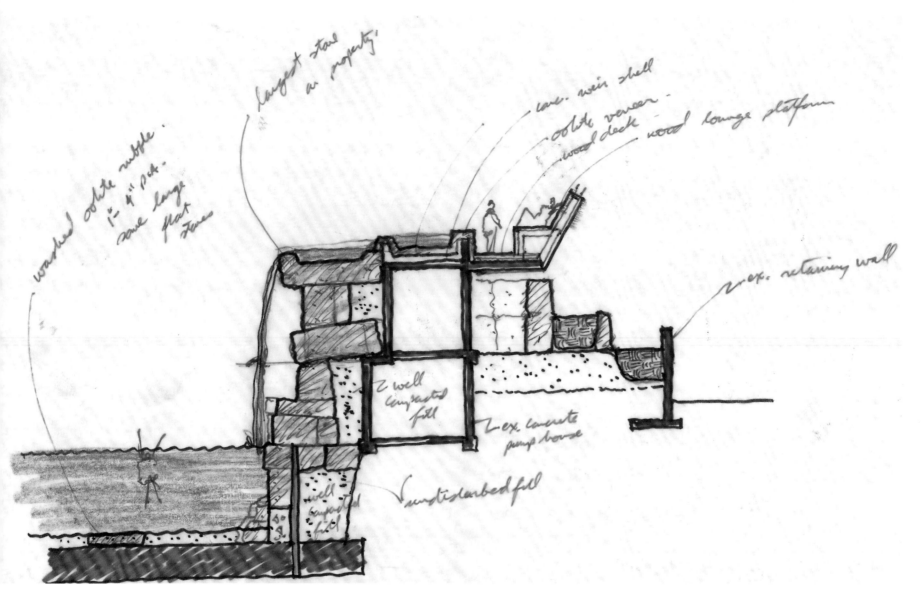

washed oolite rubble. 1"–4" pcs. some large flat stones

largest stone on property

ex. weir shell
oolite veneer
wood deck
wood lounge platform

well compacted fill

ex. retaining wall

ex. concrete pump house

undisturbed fill

well compacted fill

ABOVE A section of the waterfall that cascades into a lagoon at the property's lower ridge. The 20-foot-high stone formation also masks the pump house. When the stonework was complete, Jungles himself dove into the lagoon from the top water basin—to test the waters, of course!

RIGHT A design development planting plan for the lagoon area. One of the garden's more notable features is a 30-foot manmade oolite bluff that runs from the garden overlook to the lagoon's bottom.

PREVIOUS PAGES This man-made lagoon was constructed from oolitic limestone monoliths excavated on site. The lagoon's edge is accented by *Agave attenuata*, *Clusia rosea*, *Ernodea littoralis*, *Rhizophora mangle*, and *Suriana maritima*.

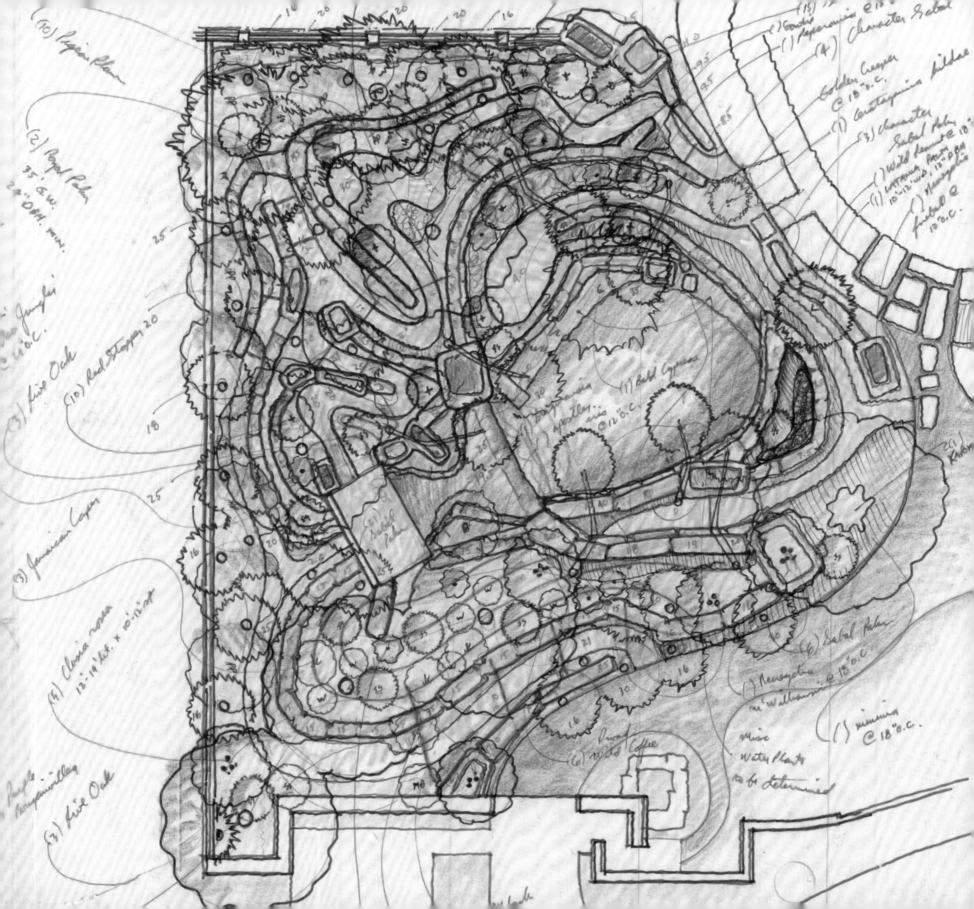

OPPOSITE, CLOCKWISE FROM TOP LEFT An entryway to the "mango court" features *Quercus virginiana* and *Dioon mejiae* to the right of its wooden gates and *Chonemorpha fragrans* along the top of its pergola. A path runs along the back elevation of the lagoon's stone formation, linking it to off-street parking and the waterfront lot. This *Mangifera indica* once straddled the property line; now it shades common ground between the united property's two main houses, and is surrounded by *Dypsis lanceolata*, climbing *Philodendron* sp., and *Portea* 'Jungles.' The waterfront lot faces Biscayne Bay, and includes a small boathouse, a helicopter pad, and a dock.

ABOVE An excavated oolite bluff shows the property's original grade. The *Ficus benghalensis* was once on four separate properties, which have now been acquired by the same owner.

FAR LEFT A view from the cantilevered pool cascade at dusk. The architecture was inspired by the work of Roberto Burle Marx.

LEFT A path of oolite stone leads to the property's historic residence, which was once home to both William Jennings Bryan and Robert Frost. The pool, by Proun Space Studio, features a swim lane that extends below the cantilevered terrace.

RIGHT The grotto was designed to capture water and to protect the house's basement from flooding. *Acoelorrhaphe wrightii* creates a canopy above a stone pathway featuring vibrant *Cordyline fruticosa* 'Peter Buck' and *Philodendron* 'Burle Marx.'

FAR RIGHT Four separate carved and reinforced oolite monoliths expand the water's presence in the garden by providing cascades from various elevations.

PREVIOUS PAGES A path of rough-hewn stones leads to an elevated multiuse platform with built-in stone seats and custom cushions—a space perfect for private concerts. Plantings include *Adansonia digitata*, *Costus comosus*, *Microsorum scolopendrium*, and *Sabal palmetto*.

The stewards of Golden Rock Inn, artists Helen and Brice Marden, were attracted to this former eighteenth-century sugar plantation on a quiet, 36-square-mile Caribbean island for the abundance of living things that were sharing its grounds, such as green vervet monkeys, hummingbirds, tree frogs, sheep, goats, and donkeys. Its natural setting is also dramatic and breathtaking; it is perched 1,000 feet above sea level on the lower side of Mount Nevis, a towering but inactive volcano. Their collaboration with Jungles created a mountainside retreat for the soul that feels organic and whole. Volcanic boulders direct the site hydrology, terrace the soil, and catch the tropics' ethereal light. Almost unspeakably romantic views toward Montserrat and Antigua are framed through sculpted ficus trees. All the elements that define the art of garden creation are in harmony here: light, stone, water, plants, structure, landform, and sky.

The artists' love of lush, wild vegetation prompted Jungles to design with indigenous species as well as colorful subtropical species from around the world. The remote location dictated using local contractors who would be knowledgeable about sourcing local plants and arranging for international shipments of any additional plant material. Prior to beginning the project, he assembled a team of local nursery owners, landscapers, builders, and stonemasons. All the materials had to be delivered up makeshift roads with steep inclines—and around free-grazing animals.

Both artists worked directly with Jungles on different aspects of the garden's design. He and Helen curated the plant selection with an overall aesthetic in mind, and favored unusual and exceptional specimen cycads and succulents to make it a reality. Brice collaborated with him and the on-site implementation specialist, Dave Schroeder, to set unearthed boulders. These were arranged in different locations to create inviting destinations where guests could circulate and experience the garden. Boulders too large to move were simply uncovered and allowed to be appreciated for their own monumental scale.

Other boulders, stones, and pebbles unsettled during the process of creating necessary roads, parking areas, and terraces for a new restaurant were saved and sorted according to size. These were later arranged to retain steep slopes, build steps, direct water, or to create pockets of microclimates for certain plants. Five large boulders discovered during the excavation of a new wing for the restaurant and initially shoved unceremoniously off to one side hinted, serendipitously, at what was to become the garden's signature element: an area dubbed "The Rocks."

Terraced, placid lily ponds grace a new dining area around "The Rocks," and water trickles in a gentle cascade down a historic wall that once directed water to the original plantation houses' cistern—restored to collect precipitation for use in irrigating the new garden. The water pours from a wall-top rill onto an unearthed, sculpted boulder and then flows lazily into a grotto.

The overall garden also required several basic improvements to make it suitable for use by guests. Circulation to the resort's rental cottages needed to be made passable and memorable, so Jungles created meandering pathways to and between them that play with both intimate and grand moments. Runoff from the mountainside was redirected to improve site hydrology—to retention areas blanketed in thick grasses and wide-leafed alocasias. The ravine's slopes needed to be stabilized, so Jungles took the opportunity to enhance them with textured and colorful plantings, which in turn draw attention to the unique property's centuries-old ruins.

ABOVE A section depicting the hillside entry sequence for hotel and restaurant guests. Retaining walls made of large boulders and dense plantings mask the cuts into the topography and conceal parked vehicles from patrons' views above.

RIGHT Necessary site grading produced a treasure trove of boulders. These massive rocks were unearthed for dramatic effect at points throughout the property. The most unique boulder was selected for use in the water element.

OPPOSITE Locally available plants and those to be imported to the small island are indicated on a master planting plan.

PREVIOUS PAGES Mount Nevis in cloud cover. The clients' love of exotic plants drove the inclusion of succulents such as *Aechmea* 'Dean,' *Aloe ferox*, *Beaucarnea recurvata*, *Cactaceae*, and *Pachypodium lamerei*. Jungles created an elevated hill that would provide rapid drainage for these plants.

OPPOSITE, TOP LEFT The view of the new entrance and approach road to the restaurant's parking terrace. The entry aligns with the volcano's peak, the historic plantation house, and an ancient lava-blast boulder field.

OPPOSITE, BOTTOM LEFT A verdant path was created on the site of the former kitchen service and loading area.

OPPOSITE, RIGHT The Rocks restaurant dining terrace at dusk. *Veitchia montgomeryana* are positioned in nearby planters and create a sense that the landscape matured naturally due to their great height. The new restaurant's building, terrace, and water gardens are by Edward Tuttle of Design Realization.

LEFT The garden and its views to Mount Nevis are designed to be seen from multiple vantage points. Plantings include *Alcantarea imperialis*, *Bougainvillea* 'Alabama Sunset,' *Coccothrinax crinita*, *Heliocereus*, *Sansevieria cylindrica*, and *Zoysia* spp. harvested on the island and installed as plugs.

115

FAR LEFT The pathway that leads from the dining terrace to the cottages is edged with tall stalks of *Bambusa chungii.*

LEFT A wild garden passage invites the curious to enter. *Justicia betonica, Phoenix sylvestris, Tripsacum dactyloides,* and *Zoysia* spp. line the way.

ABOVE The island's elusive mountaintop in a rare moment of clarity. Large-scale plants give the view a dramatic frame, including *Adansonia digitata, Aechmea blanchetiana* 'Orange Form,' *Coccothrinax miraguama, Dioon spinulosum, Euphorbia lactea* 'White Ghost,' and *Portulacaria afra.*

ABOVE The view from the uppermost guest cottage toward the historic sugar mill ruins and a mighty *Ceiba pentandra*. *Dioon edule*, *Encephalartos*, and *Cycus* species are planted above a broad expanse of Spartina bakeri.

RIGHT This feature repurposed a water channel atop an existing historic wall, which originally transported rainwater to a lower cistern. Jungles diverted the flow toward a newly created boulder fountain by means of an intentionally industrial-looking weir. Its sound subtly enlivens the restaurant terrace.

ABOVE An existing *Samanea saman* tree is underplanted with *Aechmea* 'Marcelino,' *Kalanchoe gastonis-bonnieri*, and *Philodendron speciosum* to create a tapestry of color and texture.

RIGHT A *Ceiba pentandra's* buttress-like roots wrap around remnants of historic sugar plantation structures. The ravine beyond experiences inundation during the rainy season, so was filled and restored with water-loving plants.

OVERLEAF, CLOCKWISE FROM TOP LEFT Reddish tones unite the trunk of *Adansonia digitata*, the broad leaves of an *Aechmea* 'Marcelino,' and the flowers of *Bougainvillea* 'Alabama Sunset.' Mottled leaves at the tight leaf base of a *Vriesea hieroglyphica*. The tufted blooms of a *Pseudobombax ellipticum* give it its common name, the shaving brush tree. A flower spike on a *Aechmea* hybrid 'Song of Linda.' Water lilies in the water garden adjacent to the restaurant. The bloom spike of an *Androlepis skinneri* bromeliad.

SIEBEL GARDEN

Jungles first interviewed the clients for this project, the Siebels, on their homesite at Baker's Bay Golf & Ocean Club, a private residential development set on the northern 585 acres of Great Guana Cay in the Abaco Islands of the Bahamas. He was greeted with a blank canvas: sandy grounds and a preserved coastal dune peppered with coppice vegetation. He was asked to create a garden that could withstand a tremendous amount of wind and salt spray—but also one that would exude enough formality to be in harmony with the architecture while at the same time imbuing the property with a gently relaxed beach house flare.

Merrill, Pastor & Colgan Architects sited the house at the edge of a 20-foot dune. The garden was then positioned on the leeward side of the two-story residence to shield it from formidable beachfront conditions. Land and sand movement provided an appealing grade change between the street and the entry walkway, so Jungles capitalized on it by creating a playful arrangement of platform steps and landings instead of the expected set of stairs. The garden pathway, which was originally envisioned by the architect as a formal, paved sidewalk that would echo the form of the house's loggia, was reimagined with island whimsy in mind. The finished walk is composed of a series of floating, rectangular slabs of indigenous stone of various sizes that lead to the front door along an organized axis. A circular driveway and parking area were positioned a short distance away from the entrance garden, which allows the arrival sequence to exude a welcoming, human scale.

The island's poor soil development and predominantly sandy substrates called for mostly native, resilient plantings. Having worked on many beachfront lots, Jungles selected plant material that would give texture, depth, and sculptural qualities to the garden. The clients are particularly passionate about color, and also hired a color consultant for the home's exterior surfaces and interior palette. Complementary hues in the landscape are introduced by fuchsia bougainvillea on vine trellises, large pink swaths of muhly grass, blooming violet water lilies, and flowering shrubs.

A pool lies to one side in front of the house; it was originally envisioned as being enclosed by a high wall but was reconfigured to be open though still visually separate from the entry walk. Low, terraced steps lined with turf separate the pool level from the walk. The approach to the house now flows together on three different levels. The pool garden's periphery is planted with dense native vegetation and boasts sculptural gumbo limbo trees that were hand-selected and sourced from a nearby coppice. Throughout the garden, large stone platforms and low stone walls were crafted from indigenous stone that resembles rammed earth; this stonework became one of the garden's most notable features.

The beachfront garden lies between the far side of the house and the ocean, enveloped in a spectrum of blues between sea and sky. A hot tub is perched just at the edge of the manmade interventions; its position allows bathers to look out over the preserved dune. A curved pathway to the dune circumvents existing thatch palms and an outdoor shower element. Narrow boardwalks floating over the dune itself provide access around the property. The garden is regularly buffeted with gusting winds and has endured two hurricanes since it was installed. As one of the first homesites completed in the community, it suggests a thoughtful approach for all future developments.

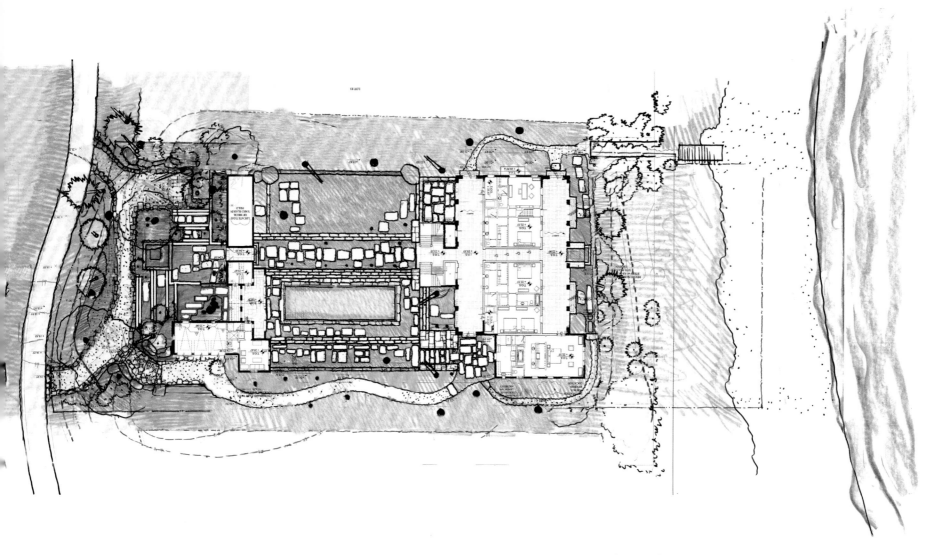

ABOVE Stone platforms and a lily pond punctuate the entry garden, which the site plan reveals to be on the main axis and aligned with the house's gate and portal to the ocean. The entry walk, pool garden, and sunken garden all fuse to create a casual, wind-protected garden space.

RIGHT An informal path leads from the entry gate to the main residence. Long platform Florida keystone steps interplanted with low grass further organize the space. Several *Cocos nucifera* trees, relocated from cleared land, complement the scale of the architecture.

FAR RIGHT The ocean portal leads to a spa perched at the edge of the dunes.

PREVIOUS PAGES Jungles often seeks out local masons when working overseas and is appreciative of their fresh, new stonework ideas. Here, low stone walls were crafted with indigenous stone reminiscent of rammed earth; beach pebbles are mixed into the veneer.

LEFT Indigenous, specimen canopy trees were relocated from cleared land. Here, the native strangler fig, *Ficus aurea*, and *Bursera simaruba*, also called American gum or American elemi, provide scale and shade.

ABOVE A view toward the pool garden from the parking area at the main residence. The overscaled platforms flanking the steps to the pool garden are covered in a unique stone veneer.

RIGHT The terrace on the second floor of the main residence overlooks the pool garden. The scale of the garden elements, planted steps, stone platforms, and ceramic pottery were designed to complement the scale of the architecture.

RIGHT Bougainvillea will eventually cover the entrance's trellis, adding additional drama to the long, direct view through the entire property and to the Atlantic Ocean beyond.

BELOW A monolith of oolite was shipped from Florida to create a water feature that provides texture and sound for the entry garden.

OPPOSITE An informal walkway of rough stone pavers leads to an extensive beach twenty feet below the dune garden.

This property, known as Gretchen's Garden, embraces 14.68 acres on beautiful Jupiter Island and comprises four property lots and four residential structures. The clients learned of Jungles's approach to creating habitats and his approach to planting after reading an editorial piece on his gardens in the *New York Times*. Intrigued, they sought him out and subsequently asked him to reinvigorate their grounds, which were underwhelming and featured a marked overuse of lawn.

To begin, Jungles performed a very complex inventory of the expanse's existing trees; these included monumental, mature *Ficus nitida* and banyan trees. The existing drive curved underneath the canopy of one particularly impressive *Ficus nitida*, but its branches grew dangerously low and constantly needed to be cut back; Jungles simply repositioned the driveway to run around the drip line of the tree. This gesture also organized the departure drive on an axis with a mighty banyan tree and cleared views to its distinctive aerial roots, which had been surrounded by miscellaneous haphazard plantings that limited the impact of its presence until the existing plants were relocated and the area was simplified with large swaths of native shrubs and groundcover. The banyan was home to a family of owls, so great care was taken not to disturb them in the process.

Other interventions included reworking areas adjacent to an existing lagoon pool. Jungles created demonstration gardens to link a renovated guest cottage—a little suburban house with a garage converted into living space—to the landscape. Guests now enter the home through a lush entrance garden and eventually arrive at a rear garden featuring a trellised vine structure and water feature. The plant palette mostly relies on native species that provide color. Jungles designed a modern subterranean structure between the banyan and the lagoon pool to house a bathroom and changing rooms, and its roof doubles as an elevated platform for dancing and entertaining. The walkways that trace the lagoon pool vary in size and formality, from floating stone pads to stone patio areas and steps.

The clients reside in the property's historic house. Although beautiful, it had an unresolved exterior spatial organization. Raymond elevated a terrace facing the water, removing cumbersome steps in the process, and created a garden and a landscape that now roll gracefully into the threshold of the house. Gentle grade transitions provide privacy from Hobe Sound and an enhanced pedestrian experience.

The gardens have evolved over time and, notably, through three major hurricanes and an on-site explosion. Jungles restored the shoreline with a stone retaining wall and dune plantings. Several destination garden rooms have been added, including a pocket beach for family bonfires and picnics. Each is located a convenient distance from the four dwellings. The swaths of lawn have gradually been reduced, and large-scale existing plant material has been relocated on-site to reveal vistas to the waterway as well.

ABOVE Once obscured by miscellaneous palm trees, a tall *Ficus benghalensis* is revealed and framed by the silver-blue foliage of *Bismarckia nobilis*.

LEFT A detail of the family "pocket beach." Plantings include *Thrinax radiata* trees and underplantings of *Spathoglottis plicata* and *Zamia furfuracea*.

OPPOSITE The driveway was relocated from this area. *Licuala grandis* and *Microsorum scolopendrium* now enjoy the shade of a mighty *Ficus nitida*.

PREVIOUS PAGES This area was once a circular, suburban-style driveway; now dense plantings separate it from adjacent parking and vine arbors, ponds, and stone paths create a more memorable procession to the front door. *Aechmea* 'Patricia,' *Neoregelia* 'Jill,' and *Trachelospermum asiaticum* 'Minima' thrive on the ground plane.

CLOCKWISE FROM TOP LEFT View sheds were established to celebrate existing legacy trees. Colorful plantings include *Agave* 'Gainesville Blue,' *Rondeletia*, and *Trachelospermum jasminoides*. The restored shoreline features *Aloe vera*, *Hibiscus rosa-sinensis*, and *Hymenocallis latifolia*. A diminutive water element composed mostly of plant material and indigenous boulders with character helps to conceal a driveway just to the left.

OPPOSITE This cap rock shoreline was previously concealed by soil and plantings. After an active hurricane season effectively cleaned it up, Jungles had the textural rock exposed along its full length to allow appreciation of its natural beauty.

This site's commanding vistas and distant landmarks, including the Cerro de las Mitras (the Hill of the Miters), suggested its name. It also lies adjacent to Chipinque National Park, a beautiful and undisturbed forest overlooking downtown Monterrey. Jungles became engaged in the project after the major earthwork interventions and architectural plans were already complete, and worked primarily to complement the house's grand scale.

The clients felt it would be important for their property to blend in with the vegetation on the mountainside. Jungles studied the language of existing plant material, a "Texas palette" of dogwoods, redbuds, and live oaks—many of the same trees he had grown up with as a child in the Midwest, in fact. Years before, the client's father had lovingly started a nursery of native trees, intending for his son to use them when he eventually built a home for himself; 95 percent of the trees used in the final gardens were sourced from this nursery. Jungles found the remaining plant material at local nurseries, and discovered along the way that he needed to create a list of botanical names for the plants he wanted because the common names varied from one part of the city to another.

On his initial visit, Jungles looked at other interesting projects in the area, including the homes of the clients' relatives. This prompted him to start a dialogue about indigenous stone and its possible applications, which wound up being used as driveway and retaining wall material.

A large section of mountainside had been cut away during construction and had been crudely coated in concrete to prevent erosion, so Jungles suggested staining the exposed concrete for a more natural appearance. He also designed an elevated planter filled with tall, native trees to mask the area and to reduce the impact of its presence in the garden.

Jungles performed several other hardscape interventions to make the steep hillside site feel welcoming. The driveway from the entrance gate, for example, had been built as a concrete bridge that ran along the side of the mountain. There, he incorporated linear planters and detailed the planting scheme to evoke a sense of driving on natural grade, not on a bridge. The lower level of the house contains children's spaces, so to give them more outdoor room, he designed a wooden deck that cantilevers over the hill. A sunken planter at the edge makes it feel as if it is on level ground, not floating 50 feet out into the open air. He also created a boardwalk to hang off the retaining walls, for ease of garden maintenance and to provide circulation to a padel tennis court.

The property's most immediately striking outdoor space may be a large lawn leading to an infinity pool that seems to drop right off the side of the mountain; this area and an adjacent summer kitchen were designed to accommodate outdoor entertaining. Colombian artist Hugo Zapata's monumental, seven-piece rock sculpture mediates the visual transition from low outdoor seating to an adjacent high window wall.

This was the firm's first project in Mexico, so it was the first time plans needed to be presented in English as well as Spanish. Designing in metric measurements proved challenging, mainly due to the site's complicated topography. Overall, the design team enjoyed working with passionate clients who enjoyed planting trees at night via headlamps, setting boulders themselves, and drinking tequila together.

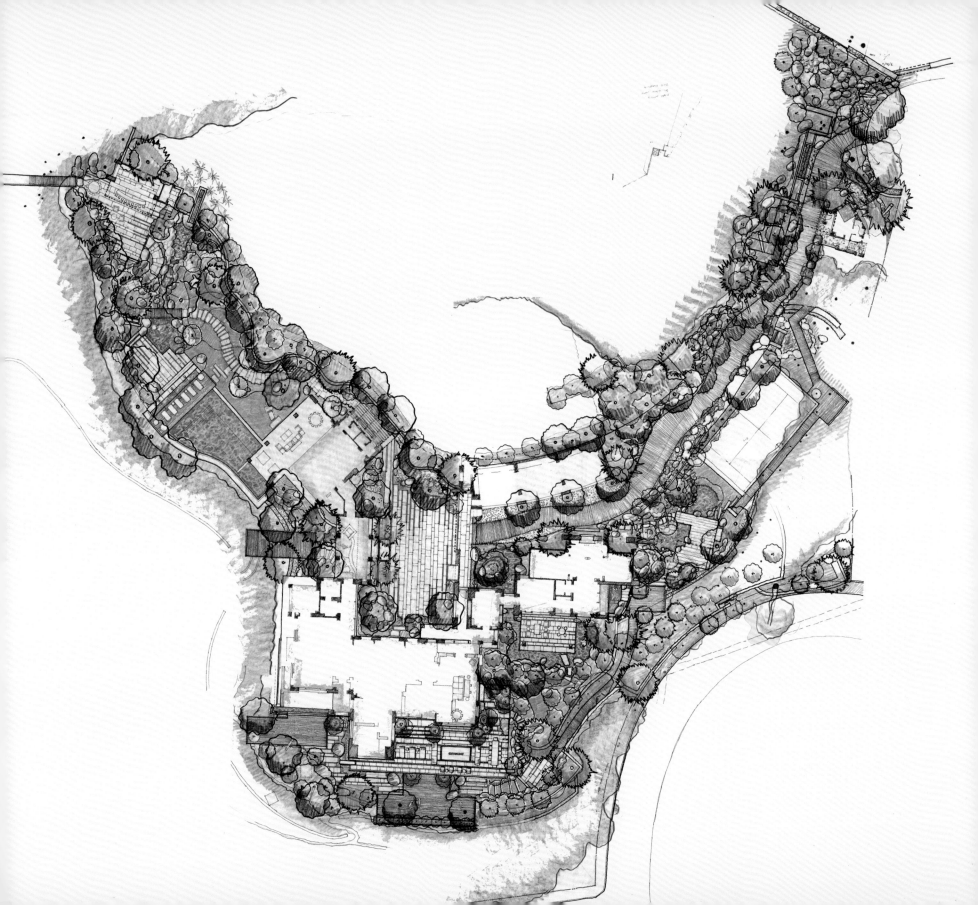

LEFT The garden design schematic shows several different garden experiences, each with its own characteristics, incorporated into this severely graded site.

ABOVE Three views showing indigenous plants and stones integrated into this Mexican garden. The concept was to link it with the surrounding forest while creating a bold and architectural feel.

PREVIOUS PAGES Architect Gustavo Medellin designed this dramatic infinity pool, consulting with Jungles on the choice of a gray-green stone liner to help it meld visually with the garden.

LEFT Three detail views of the garden, taken within a year of its completion, demonstrate the concept of "rich simplicity" that drove the overall garden's design.

TOP The lower terrace garden, which is perched above a fifty-foot drop to the reforested hillside below.

ABOVE The sprawling event lawn, incorporated to accommodate large family gatherings and social events.

RIGHT Magnificent mountains tower over the entry drive, originally designed as a bridge. Planters placed on its downhill side—and large enough to support several *Lagerstroemia indica* trees—help it feel as though it's integrated into the natural grade.

OVERLEAF, LEFT Architect Gustavo Medellin incorporated broad windows into his design for the home to take advantage of enviable views of Monterrey, then consulted with the clients and Jungles on planting details.

OVERLEAF, RIGHT A *Quercus virginiana* of special character, grown by the client's father in his personal nursery, is the centerpiece of the parking court.

LEFT The garden has a view of Cerro de las Mitras, one of the three distinctive ranges that define Monterrey. This lower terrace, immediately adjacent to the children's bedrooms, is cantilevered over the restored forest fifty feet below to provide them play space.

ABOVE In homage to Luis Barragán, Jungles created a viewing portal to the distant Cerro de las Mitras from the master bathroom's garden; this gave the entire project its name: Ventana de la Montaña.

RIGHT Early evening in the upper garden terrace. Dramatic views of all three Monterrey mountain ranges and the twinkling city lights below make it an ideal location for outdoor entertaining. The sculpture is by Colombian artist Hugo Zapata.

PREVIOUS PAGES A padel court viewing terrace surrounded by *Agapanthus*, one of Jungles's favorite plants but one he rarely gets the chance to incorporate since it is not appropriate for use in subtropical zones.

Montana's famously expansive and dynamic skies suggested a design for this vacation home that is about large yet subtle gestures. The client originally considered siting it on high ground, on a bluff overlooking "the Crazies" mountain range, a stone's throw away from a rattlesnake den and in the midst of a prairie dog town. After further consideration, Jungles and Hughes Umbanhowar Architects decided to nestle the house on the banks of a river below in order to take full advantage of the water's dynamism. This site is subject to seasonal water inundation when runoff from nearby mountains swells the river's banks, however, and in the summer, conversely, water can become scarce. The design for the site works creatively to mediate this dramatic flux. The house itself, for example, is set on a porous plinth that lifts the floors well above the flood line. To ensure that water would be plentiful even in dry season, Jungles planned for a series of spring-fed ponds to surround the house—these are now the immediate landscape's most defining feature.

The main pedestrian entry to the house gives the impression that it is floating on the surface of the water. Irregularly shaped stone pavers with grass joints lead to a pond that lies directly in front of the house. A 34-foot-long stone slab reminiscent of a drawbridge offers passage across; it is supported by a system of steel beams and gabions just below the water's surface. A recirculating, cascading water feature to the left of the stone slab activates the pond's surface and creates white noise to cover over any echoes from the highway. Boulders that Jungles sourced on site and hand selected are placed in natural-looking formations around the pond's edge—some offer seating, others provide a means for swimmers to enter and exit the water.

This main pond was already in the process of being dug by a local consultant when Jungles amended the scheme to create a small island within it that would preserve a lone cottonwood tree initially slated for removal. He decided its weathered branches would create an interesting spectacle as they cast their reflection upon the water's surface in early morning and evening light. This, in turn, prompted him to enlarge the pond and to form it into a more natural shape. Cascading streams now link a total of three ponds that surround the house.

The final planting palette celebrates the American West, and features groves of aspen and bur oak trees as well as indigenous shrubs selected for their interesting textures throughout the seasons. Meadow plantings appropriate to the riparian setting also line the ponds' banks, and any disturbed areas were regenerated with native species. These seemingly preexistent plant compositions mask the hand of the designer and encourage habitat creation for local fauna. The schematic planting layout plan was implemented by a local landscape team, with Jungles visiting periodically to lay out bed lines and to offer suggestions for additional planting enhancements between growing seasons.

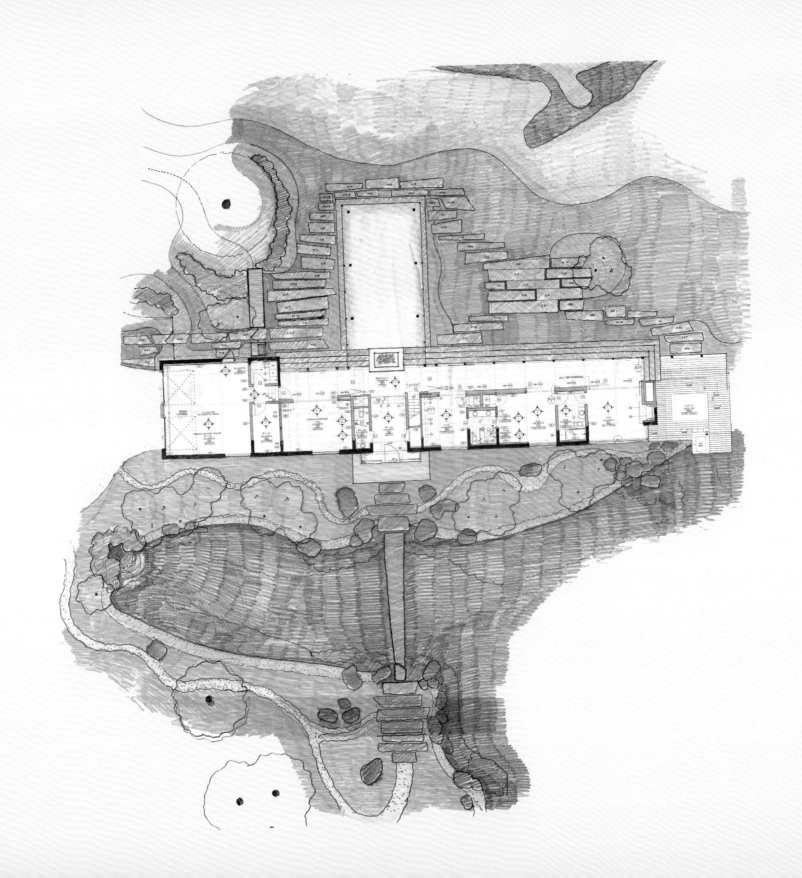

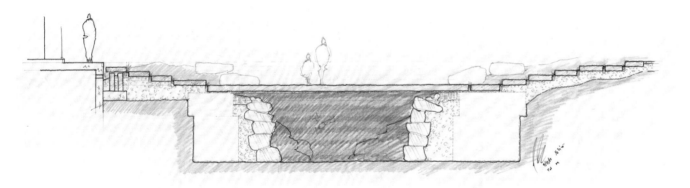

LEFT AND ABOVE Plans and a section showing the proposed pond and stone monolith bridge. The footpath pavers are of stone the client had already obtained.

PREVIOUS PAGES An elevated fire pit at the edge of the house adds drama to a garden designed to look as wild as the surrounding Montana countryside.

OVERLEAF A sodded roof helps the house blend with the surrounding landscape. Fields adjacent to the residence and the ponds' edges were also seeded with native grasses and wildflowers. The gnarled cottonwood tree at right was saved by Jungles during construction with the intent of creating an island around it; now it has become a favorite destination for swimmers.

FAR LEFT Stone monoliths, laid together in an informal-yet-contemporary way, create a terrace seating area next to the house designed by Hughes Umbanhowar Architects.

LEFT A pond near the river that runs next to the house was created as part of the view shed toward "the Crazies" mountains, as seen from the master bedroom's terrace.

ABOVE Rough-textured stone creates a dramatic 34-foot-long bridge to the front entry. The island at left was created to help the landscape feel mature and natural. Mostly native, non-showy plants were chosen to help the site blend with the wilderness surrounding it, and were selected with the help of local nursery owner Sandi Blake of Blake Nursery. Plant compositions were created to enhance the landscape on both visual and ecological levels.

TOP The entry vestibule contains broad windows to invite the famous Montana sky inside.

ABOVE The master bedroom's terrace was positioned to take advantage of views over both the water and the mountains.

RIGHT Three ponds on the property are linked to accommodate seasonal fluctuations in water flow. This "middle pond" features banks that are sodded with indigenous plants.

OVERLEAF A meandering, processional entry drive from the highway and along the periphery of farm fields that cover much of this 2,000-acre-ranch's land creates a sense of gradual discovery. A substantially graded road features strategic turns that lengthen view sheds to the surrounding natural focal points and leads visitors down and through the undulating landscape.

GROVENOR ROOFTOP GARDEN

Ella Fontanals-Cisneros, design advocate, art collector, and philanthropist extraordinaire, persuaded us to take on the design of her private residential garden. "The sky's the limit," she said—and she meant it. The site is thirty-four stories above Coconut Grove's main boulevard, and lies just across from Sailboat Bay.

The views from the 2,543-square-foot, L-shaped rooftop are spectacular, if dizzying. We developed the program for the garden in conjunction with Ella and Spanish interior designer Luis Bustamante. The team decided to make it a cozy, secure space with human-scale proportions, plantings as lush as the high winds and glaring sun would allow, low-maintenance and drought-tolerant landscape materials, and accommodation for intimate groups as well as for gatherings of fifty or more.

The rooftop's most prominent feature—and originally its most obtrusive—was a 15-foot-square pool. Jungles corrected its proportions by lengthening it, then added a wide lounging edge created of stepped îpe-wood platforms. These diminish the pool's visual mass as well as provide water access. An infinity edge pulls the pool's surface taut. Water cascades over its perimeter, splashing down a vertical, tiled surface into a basin four feet below. An adjacent wall of stacked stones acts as a water feature during the day; at night it mimics the view of city lights in the distance as thousands of fiber optic filaments placed between the stacked stones twinkle. Two massive columns on the bayfront facade of the building rise above roof level; we sculpted them to allow for ease of circulation around the pool area.

The îpe-wood pool shell, elevated deck, and platform steps create a datum line against the exterior walls. The same wood wraps a private service kitchen with a dumbwaiter near the dining area as well as a new storage cabinet that doubles as an elevated planter. An aluminum trellis sympathetic to the vocabulary of the building's architecture covers these areas and features a retractable awning to mediate sun exposure.

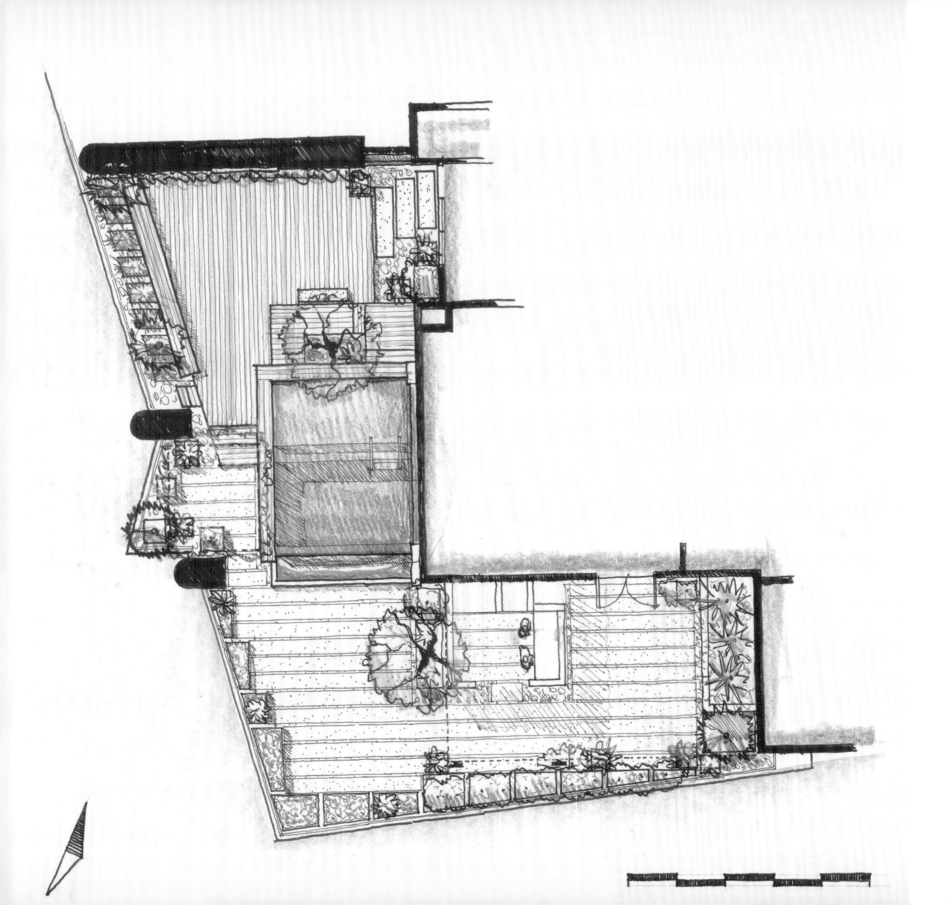

OPPOSITE Three discrete spaces were planned for this rooftop space: a lounging area, a pool, and a dining terrace.

LEFT, ABOVE Stacked stone wall finishes, wood paneling, glass doors, and powder-coated custom aluminum planters were introduced to help make the soaring rooftop space feel human-scaled and welcoming.

LEFT, BELOW The trellis shelters an outdoor kitchen and dining area, provides a scale transition from the residential tower's bulky terminus, and supports a retractable awning. Service spaces are shielded from view behind îpe-wood slats.

PREVIOUS PAGES The view toward downtown Miami is the roof garden's most distinctive feature. *Alcantarea imperialis* and *Bulbine frutescens* embellish seating areas positioned to take full advantage of it.

ABOVE *Sansevieria cylindrica* and *Bulbine frutescens* line the exterior railing. Beyond lies the City of Miami's Marina at Sailboat Bay.

RIGHT Water cascades down the length of a stacked-slate wall and into the pool. One *Bucida molineti* tree is provided for scale, and is under-planted with low species including *Sansevieria masoniana* 'Whale Fin' and *Bulbine frutescens*, which add color without obstructing the view.

ABOVE Plant interventions, such as this custom tillandsia installation on stainless-steel mesh by horticulturalist Jennifer Davit, soften the building's stucco surfaces.

RIGHT *Kalanchoe thyrsiflora* 'Silver Platter,' with its thin and upright stalks, emulates the Miami skyline beyond.

OPPOSITE The outdoor dining room features materials—wood, metal, steel, stone, and large plants—intended to create a comfortable, relaxed ambience that shields visitors somewhat from strong rooftop breezes.

ABOVE The dining area's high trellis features an automated overhead awning that extends to shade the space for daytime dining and protects against precipitation while leaving view corridors wide open.

OPPOSITE Fiber-optic lights embedded in the stacked-slate water wall twinkle at night, creating a dialogue with the lights of downtown Miami beyond.

PAVILION BEACH CLUB GARDEN

St. Kitts, West Indies | 2011

This 3-acre beach club sits within the larger Christophe Harbour private ownership development, a 2,500-acre luxury property on the southeast peninsula of St. Kitts—an island with terrain often compared to that of the South Pacific. The design was driven by the goals of creating a sheltered place for relaxation and enjoying views of verdant topography and a crescent-shaped beach. The development company's director of design and planning selected Jungles after seeing an image of a beachfront residential pool he had previously designed in the Bahamas. Since the office was engaged early in the design process, Jungles helped the architect elevate the open-air dining room to 20.5 feet to maximize views, and to site additional structures away from the beachfront, to avoid distracting from the horizon line.

The Pavilion's pool sits at a final elevation of 18 feet; Jungles designed it with an infinity edge 7 feet above the height of the dune vegetation below, which averages an elevation of 10 feet, to shield swimmers from the sight of beachgoers walking along the shore. To keep the view back into the Pavilion lush for beachgoers too, Jungles obscured the pool's high edge with boulders and cascading, resilient groundcover.

Materials—specifically flagstone—marry the interior and exterior spaces. It appears as a veneer on the architectural structures and as a paving material on the garden pathways and pool deck. Three-inch-thick slabs transition from mortar joints to grass joints as the stones move away from the built spaces and into the open. From the beach bar, club members can follow these pathways as they meander through existing seagrape trees to intimate pocket beaches for private sunbathing.

The club is located in the remnant of a dry forest zone. This means it is subject to high evaporation rates and an average annual precipitation of 34 inches. The existing site was once heavily forested— and subsequently was a burned area with beach vegetation occurring only intermittently along the shoreline. With this in mind, Jungles selected plant material that could withstand the challenging environment. Coconut palms are subject to lethal yellowing, so he selected disease-resistant cultivars and mixed the species of palms found throughout the grounds. The majority of plant material was sourced and shipped by barge from Homestead, Florida, in 40-foot flat racks and refrigerated containers.

A series of shallow retention basins was created for erosion control and paspalum grass was seeded to stabilize landforms. Soil disturbed during on-site construction was sifted to obtain material for stone walls; non-sifted soil was used for infill. Jungles engaged local contractors to set locally sourced boulders and to lay out and install plant material, communicating with the team through redlined photographs and comments on weekly site progress.

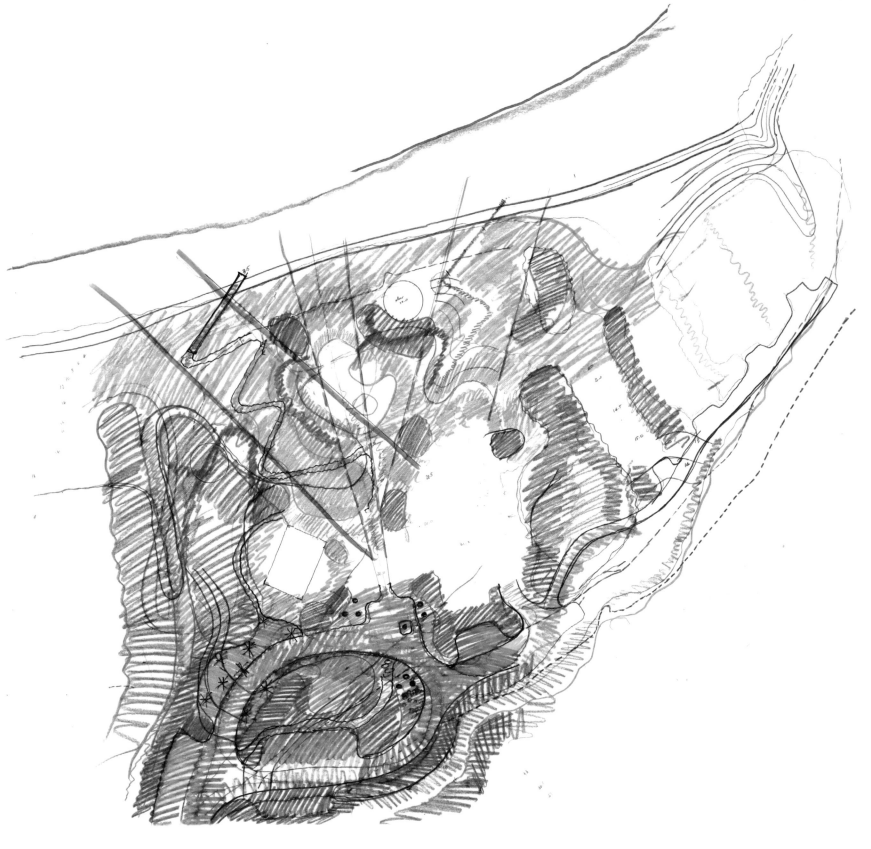

LEFT An early study of the view sheds from the entry pavilion and along the garden's central axis.

ABOVE Pavilion Beach Club is nestled within Sandy Bank Bay, a dramatic horse-shoe bay with a natural sand bank celebrated for its views to the Atlantic Ocean.

PREVIOUS PAGES The garden was designed in part to direct views from the club's entry pavilion toward Sandy Bank Bay.

ABOVE Boulders excavated during the construction of the club's structures are reused on-site as sculptural seating to evoke a sense of permanence. Multiple view sheds were created or accentuated in this area.

RIGHT One of two access paths to the beach. Indigenous plants were selected to line them whenever possible, but are supplemented with other ecologically appropriate species.

ABOVE A view back toward the island, from the infinity-edge pool to the garden's main pavilion.

RIGHT Bands of Florida cap rock, the hardest Florida stone, line the tall infinity-edge pool. Water trickles down over it and to the lower pool basin.

FAR RIGHT The limestone pool deck is staggered to create both dry and wet lounging areas. The pool features a pebble finish that helps it meld visually with the bay and ocean beyond.

This exhibition, entitled *Brazilian Modern*, was designed to display orchids in a way that reflects the spirit and tropical vibrancy of present-day Brazil. Jungles was a student and friend of the late Roberto Burle Marx, so it seemed natural to create this exhibition in his honor and to infuse it with design principles and details inspired by "the father of the modern garden."

Consequently, colorful plants were grouped together to represent the way great swaths of one species are often found in nature, and plants with particularly unique natural characteristics were displayed in ways that would draw attention to those distinctive features. In total, more than 8,000 orchids abounding with blooms were displayed in theatrical ways—dripping overhead like living chandeliers, climbing up walls, and lining ponds in cheerful masses. Vibrant color-and-texture-blocked displays, structures composed of epiphytic orchids, and cubist planters presented many different specimens as living art. This temporary orchid show introduced New York to the freedom, the boldness, and the clarity common in contemporary Brazilian garden design.

This was the New York Botanical Garden's seventh annual orchid show, though the first designed by a professional landscape architect—the previous exhibitions were executed by in-house horticulturalists. The show ran for just six weeks but attracted over 100,000 visitors to the Enid A. Haupt Conservatory. Its famous galleries provided a controlled environment for the orchids and space for grand-scale installations.

Four hanging "chandeliers" with diameters of 6 feet were filled with *Philodendron giganteum*, selected for its enormous leaves and bold texture; fuchsia, purple, and lavender orchids cascaded out from beneath them and danced just above visitors' heads. Each arrangement was planted to create a tapered, ombré effect: specimens with the most vibrant colors and largest blooms appeared at the top and the finest-textured and lightest-colored orchids hung beneath.

Burle Marx's work was directly referenced in several ways. His vertical plantings, for example, were recalled here by a 12-inch-thick, 8-foot-high, and 25-foot-long recessed panel that featured a sculptural staghorn fern set off by a background of over 600 white phalaenopsis orchids. Plant "sculptures" composed of between five and seven *Alcantarea imperialis* bromeliads and epiphytic, silver tillandsia orchids were perched at various levels throughout the exhibition space. Several *Alcantarea* species also spilled from these, onto the ground, and across the gallery to emulate their natural growth habits. Cubist-inspired planters were staggered vertically in intervals up to 13 feet high, and were filled with billowing *Alcantarea imperialis*, *Alcantarea imperialis* 'Rubra,' and pha-laenopsis orchids. An 8-by-17-foot Roberto Burle Marx ceramic mural composed of 1,325 individually painted tiles was suspended vertically above a dark-bottomed pool of calm water that reflected the colorful blooms surrounding it and visually expanded the exhibition space. Reproductions of several of Burle Marx's acrylic paintings from Jungles's personal collection were also displayed on stretched fabric canvases, introducing another dimension of his creativity to visitors.

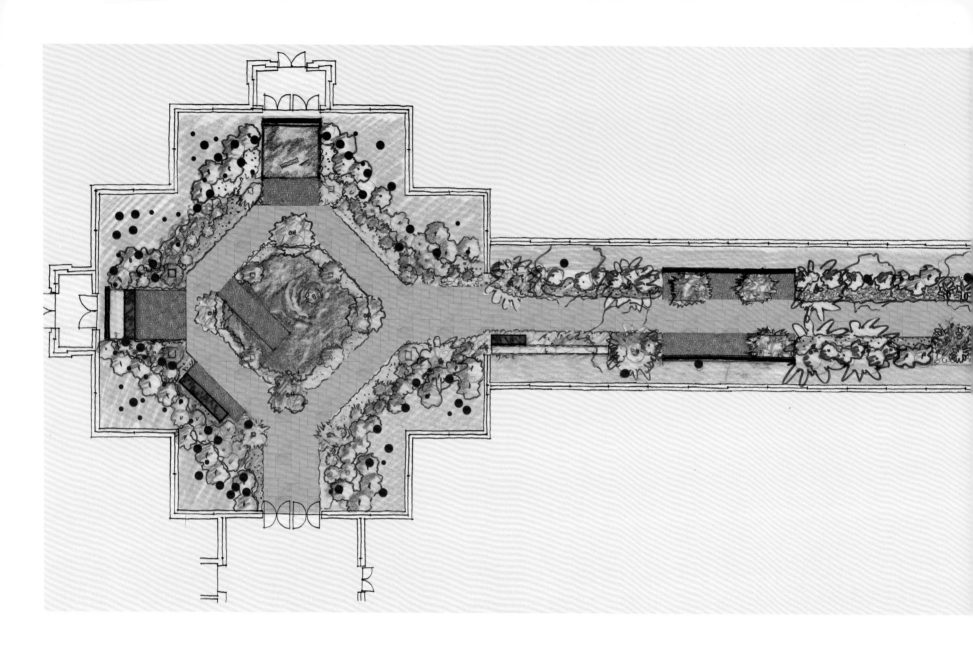

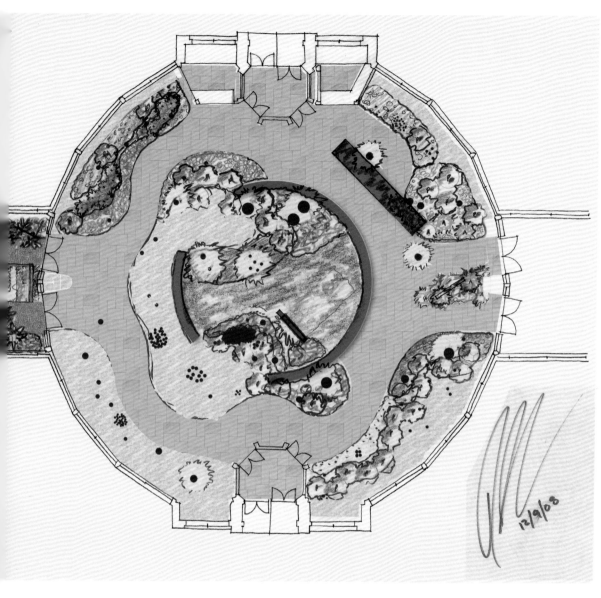

LEFT Jungles's design intended to maximize the role of the plants and orchids within the Victorian-style glass conservatory while minimizing the impact of the narrow structure. Many distinct experiences were created along the main path, and art by Roberto Burle Marx was fully integrated into the show.

ABOVE Presentation graphics produced during the design process show how abundant the plant life was intended to feel. As executed, plants completely dominated the available space and, indeed, almost took over the narrow exhibition hall completely.

PREVIOUS PAGES This Burle Marx mosaic, circa 1991, was loaned to the New York Botanical Garden by Jungles and exhibited above a reflecting pool under the conservatory's 90-foot-high glass dome. A special team from Burle Marx & Cia. in Rio—led by Julio Ono, the son of Burle Marx's business partner—installed the mural for its New York debut.

TOP Reproductions of art by Burle Marx, owned by Jungles, created visual points of interest that led patrons through the exhibit.

ABOVE A reflecting pond was introduced to magnify the impact of the orchid chandeliers, art, and the participants.

RIGHT Vertical planters modeled after Burle Marx's own designs were incorporated into the very narrow gallery.

OPPOSITE Jungles designed a white *Phalaenopsis* wall that featured a large, 35-year-old *Platycerium bifurcatum* at its center.

SOHO BEACH HOUSE GARDEN

Miami Beach, Florida | 2010

The Soho Beach House hotel and private club is the Miami extension of the London-based Soho House Group brand. The project involved a restoration and retrofit of the historic Sovereign Hotel, a landmarked 1940s Art Deco building, along with construction of a new 15-story oceanfront tower. The property's entertaining spaces include two pools, indoor and outdoor entertainment areas, elevated gardens, and a restaurant that is open to the public.

Jungles designed the open-air garden spaces to complement the beautiful and bold lines of the new tower and the original Art Deco building, and also worked to create a sense of unity between the interior and exterior environments. The overall effect conjures a "beach chic" oasis in this densely populated portion of the city. Garden spaces undulate the length of the property, and culminate at the public beach boardwalk and sand dunes.

The landscape design for Soho House focused more on creating intricate outdoor spaces than on showcasing plant diversity. Jungles was restricted to using only native plants in the easternmost beachside portion of the garden except for existing coconut palms, which he was allowed to reposition. An intense and intimate-yet-relaxing mood is exuded by all parts of the garden, from the beachfront plantings of the Beach Garden to the tree canopies above the restaurant.

Specimen silver buttonwood trees, along with a trellis structure and a 100-foot-long retractable awning, provide shade and scale for the public restaurant. Thick vines cover and hang from the trellis, positioning diners in a lush and verdant environment. Elsewhere on the grounds, native salt-tolerant plants include specimen Sabal palms, Spanish stoppers, green thatch palms, and seagrapes.

Jungles used a code requiring that the fill generated by the excavation of the new tower's foundation remain on site to his advantage, and dispersed the material to create private garden areas on different levels throughout the property. Elevated gardens border the public boardwalk along the perimeter of the Beach Garden and one side of the minimalist, rectangular pool in the Pool Garden. The 100-foot-long pool itself, designed by Jungles, sits above the ground plane, which allows water to trickle over all four sides—the mirrorlike surface seems to float in the space. Ample communal lounge furniture provides opportunities for sunbathing, and semiprivate garden and cabana areas offer spaces for small gatherings.

Overall, this project's main challenge was that only very limited areas were available for truly transformative landscape interventions. Much of the ground plane was earmarked for people, furniture, and functions—the hotel's private club regularly programs local music, fashion, and art events in the Beach Garden and Pool Garden. Nevertheless, the final design feels luxurious and enveloping.

ABOVE The view of the garden as seen from the public boardwalk. The new 15-story tower was designed by Miami-based architect Allan Shulman. All of the vegetation was added to the existing site.

RIGHT A concrete stairway poetically surrounded by an envelope of lush, indigenous greenery leads to the members-only, second-floor club. The wooden walkway leads to the public boardwalk and the beach beyond.

FAR RIGHT The view from the eighth floor shows how surrounded the pool is by dense plantings, which furthers the mission of Soho Beach House: to be a private refuge amid showier neighboring hotels.

PREVIOUS PAGES The pool garden in the early morning. This space transforms to accommodate floating stages, fashion runways, and even pool parties featuring inflatable canoes. Two specimen *Conocarpus erectus* var. *sericeus* trees separate the private pool garden from the public restaurant garden. Jungles worked closely with interior design firm Martin Brudnizki Design Studio on all of the entertaining spaces.

ABOVE Cecconi's Restaurant, open to the public, exemplifies human-scale comfort in an institutional setting. A retractable awning provides protection from rain, and specimen *Conocarpus erectus* var. *sericeus* and an improvised wood pergola provide visual warmth and texture.

RIGHT The beach garden, a popular venue for private events and weddings, was created with beach sand excavated on site—and required to remain on site by code. Jungles conceived of this space as a "pocket beach." The bar features a planted roof.

HAMMOCK GARDEN

Coral Gables, Florida | 2001

This site is magical. It is a place to experience the now; a sanctuary for humans and animals alike. Located on a 3-acre parcel perched on South Florida's highest ridge, the Hammock Garden is bounded by eight adjacent residences and fronts a historic highway. The created landscape reflects the character of an undisturbed natural landscape found within adjacent Matheson Hammock, a Miami-Dade County park planned and designed by noted landscape architect William Lyman Phillips. Two acres of existing lawn were removed and grade manipulations and excavations undertaken to expose the oolitic substrate, creating distressed rock outcrops ranging from a few feet to twenty feet in height, and solution holes of varying size and form within the landscape.

The pond is actually the water table; it fluctuates from season to season and tide to tide. Kingfishers, herons, and hawks stalk crustaceans and fish, while flocks of migratory fowl linger in the trees and open spaces. Pleasant water sounds offer surprises from unexpected places; a wispy, 20-foot cascade tumbles down a verdant cliff into a sinkhole, for example.

The bottom of the property once bordered wetlands and red mangrove forests. Fill and monoliths from the pond dig were used in landforms throughout the garden, creating privacy and providing drama. The plantings are mostly indigenous, with cypress, pond apples, and red mangrove in the pond as well as in the basin 4 feet above. Accent plants including a sculptural kapok, South American oil palm, talipot, and Bailey palm from Cuba, to name a few, are distributed among thick, indigenous species.

The ponds and water courses that were created were enhanced with littoral zone and emergent zone plantings of native species, creating a series of microclimates and habitats. Streams link various scaled ponds and help the water gently work its way back to its natural level. Cascades, streams, and basins are fed by a 2-horsepower pump. The upper pond was detailed to create a primitive, agrarian feeling.

Blocks of stone were interwoven to support radical grade changes. Surfaces are pervious; all rainwater is directed to swales and retention areas planted with moisture-loving plants. Paths and planting areas were mulched and topped with pine straw with future generations of soil in mind. These massive boulders sculpted from oolitic limestone bedrock were influenced by formations in Roberto Burle Marx's gardens.

The significance of this project lies in its extraordinary manipulation of the land to create a naturalized habitat possessing the inherent values of the natural subtropical landscapes of the Everglades and Big Cypress National Preserve.

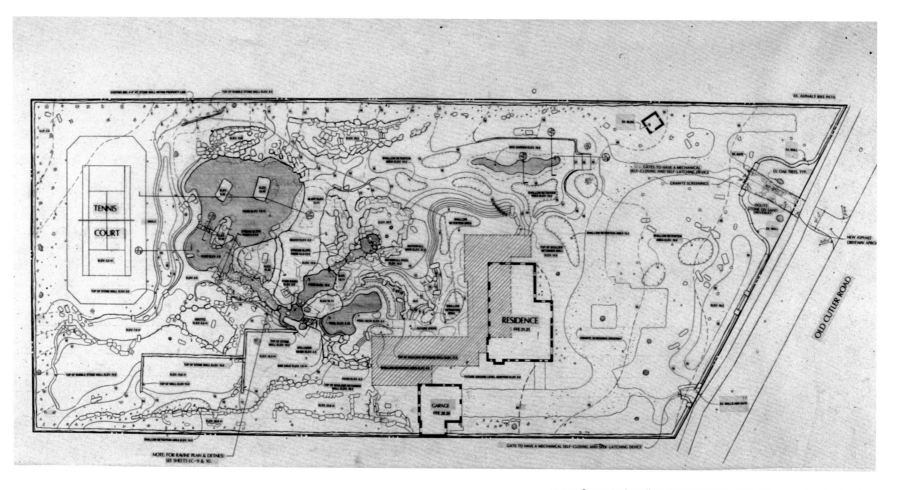

ABOVE Conceptual grading plan showing the idea of a processional water element originating at a *Taxodium distichum* slew.

RIGHT A grotto originally built for the owner's pet hog, Virginia. Plantings include *Bambusa malingensis*, *Pitcairnia angustifolia*, *Sabal palmetto*, and *Stenochlaena tenuifolia*.

PREVIOUS PAGES This is the location of an earlier pool, created in an area where stone was quarried to construct the property's original 1920s residence. The twenty-foot cascade tumbles down a cliff thriving with ferns.

ABOVE *Acacia seyal* trees, like this one from Sítio Burle Marx, have unique branching habits. Its angular forms contrast pleasantly with the leaves of the indigenous *Chrysobalanus icaco* 'Horizontal' shrub in the foreground.

RIGHT The garden is wild by design. *Heliocereus* drapes over huge oolite stone monoliths, excavated on site and arranged for drama, that appear to float over large swaths of *Ernodea littoralis* ground cover.

RIGHT A retaining wall composed of oolite boulder monoliths excavated on site creates a pleasant perch for two.

FAR RIGHT Excavated stone monoliths are placed among indigenous flowering shrubs and wildflowers; these abut a water fill that terminates at the garden's lower pond.

ABOVE The lower pond, dug into the water table, fluctuates in depth from season to season and tide to tide. The site was once a sloping lawn beneath a mango orchard.

RIGHT The upper pond basin was detailed to create a primitive feeling. The land's previous owner, a farmer, dammed the water flow to create a reservoir.

OPPOSITE Virginia's Memorial Garden. Jungles's clients desired to memorialize their pet hog with this small space.

JUNGLES STUDIO GARDEN

Miami, Florida | 2005–2015

About thirteen years ago, the studio began to occupy the second floor of an industrial building that, in its previous life, had functioned as an awning warehouse. It was surrounded exclusively by asphalt and hard surfaces. This "concrete jungle," however, was full of potential. The building is positioned on the riverside lot at an angle, which gave enough waterfront space to create a verdant oasis on this little bend in the Miami River between the high-rises that dot the riverfront and the freeway behind.

Jungles let habitat creation drive his design, selecting native palms and shade trees to demonstrate their potential for success even in urban areas. As the garden grew in over time, a microclimate emerged for his studio's enjoyment. Patina-stained concrete pavers lead to an area where river views are framed by Sabal palm trunks adorned with flowering orchids and epiphytes. Lunch hours and impromptu meetings are held underneath two distinctive shade sails designed by the late Barry McCarthy of Bamboobarry Outdoor Living. Welcome distractions occur here, from occasional manatee encounters to visits from weathered shrimp boats returning from a hard day's work.

The garden has low maintenance needs; in fact, it is intentionally left unkempt and allowed to grow unchecked to celebrate the wild side of Raymond Jungles, Inc.; it's like a three-dimensional calling card that advertises the firm's preference for designing wild gardens rather than manicured. The studio garden's lighting, in turn, shows how fixtures and light levels might be used in projects. After a hurricane killed an invasive Brazilian peppertree at the end of the street, Jungles decided to extend the garden into the public realm. Now a substantial portion of the adjacent Miami River shoreline has a more indigenous look that replicates what vegetation most likely existed here before manmade interventions.

Since the firm established its practice at this location, public opinion of the Miami River has changed tremendously. The neighborhood used to be considered a derelict area on the outskirts of the Brickell neighborhood and on the fringe of the Little Havana community. Today, the real estate market has deemed river frontage a hot commodity. Developers are beginning to redefine the riverfront as an upscale, vibrant, and livable district. The office is actively contributing to the river's revitalization and has recently been engaged to participate in a mixed-use project consisting of four tall residential towers, a public river walk, and the reimagining of Jose Marti Park. This project will set a high bar for thoughtfulness in all future Miami River developments.

ABOVE The office as seen from across the Miami River. When the studio moved here, there was not a tree in sight. Native *Sabal palmetto* and *Bursera simaruba* trees now provide habitat and shade.

RIGHT The concept plan, which identifies native Florida species that could thrive on the urban site.

PREVIOUS PAGES Once an area covered completely in asphalt, this verdant oasis is now what boaters see while cruising down the Miami River—and what clients see when visiting the office.

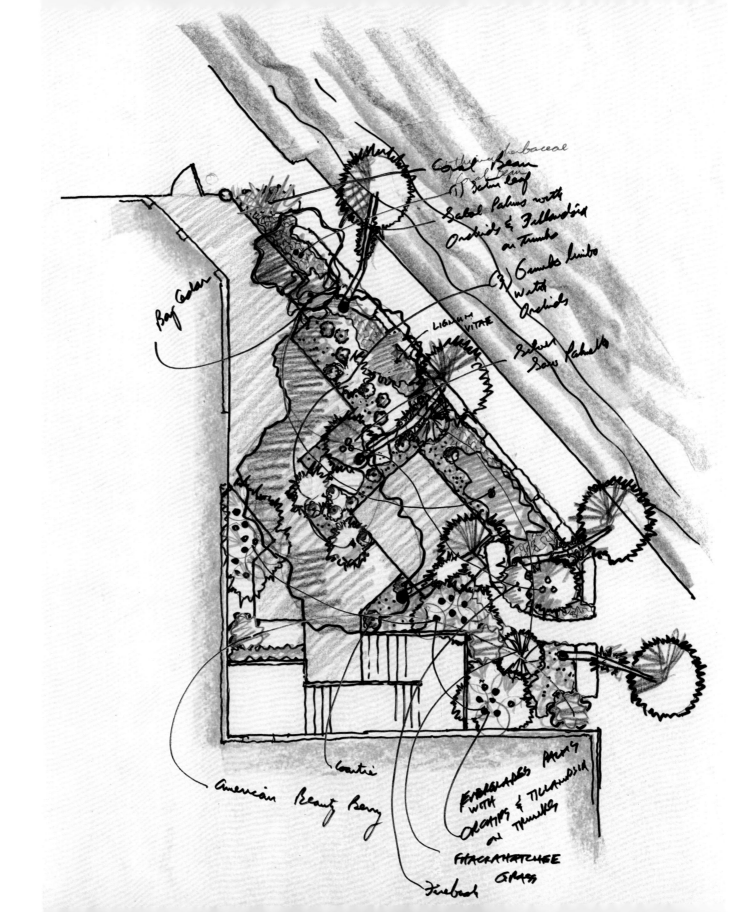

Bay Cedar

American Beauty Berry

Coontie

Fireback

FAKAHATCHEE GRASS

EVERGLADES PALMS WITH ORCHIDS & TILLANDSIA ON TRUNKS

LIGNUM VITAE

Coastal Beam
Coastal Bay
Silver Bay

Sabal Palms with Orchids & Tillandsia on Trunks

Gumbo Limbo with Orchids

Silver Saw Palmetto

RIGHT, ABOVE The view from the upstairs balcony at the studio's entrance. The staff describes the style of the garden as "industrial wild."

RIGHT, BELOW The view to the east, toward Brickell Avenue and downtown Miami. Studio staff conduct outdoor meetings and enjoy lunch hours from this vantage point.

OPPOSITE A signature vine used in Jungles projects, *Clerodendrum splendens*, grows through the entry staircase. This particular plant was brought as a seed from Sítio Burle Marx. It attracts hummingbirds and butterflies. *Acoelorrhaphe wrightii* trunks, in the background, are adorned with orchids.

WORKS IN PROGRESS

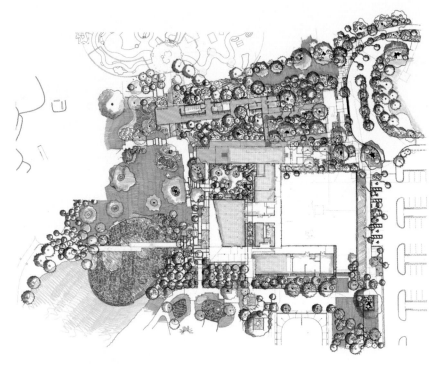

NAPLES BOTANICAL GARDEN VISITOR CENTER GARDEN

Naples, Florida

Completed in October 2014

In conjunction with LakelFlato Architects

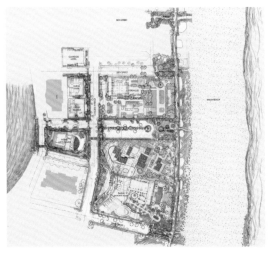

FAENA DISTRICT MASTER PLAN

Miami Beach, Florida

Slated for completion in 2016

RJI is designing the gardens of this district, from the individual project gardens to the linking streetscapes and the public improvement areas. The firm is honored to be working on the Faena House with Foster + Partners; on the Faena Art Center, Faena Bazaar, Artist-in-Residence Center, and Faena Park (a state-of-the-art automated parking complex) with Rem Koolhaas and OMA; and the Faena Saxony Hotel with Catherine Martin and Baz Luhrmann of Bazmark.

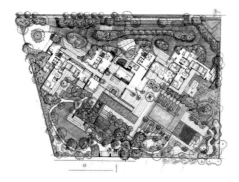

EL ALEAR GARDEN
San Pedro Garza García, Nuevo León, Monterrey, Mexico
Completed Spring 2015
A multifamily residential development in conjunction with
Landa Architects

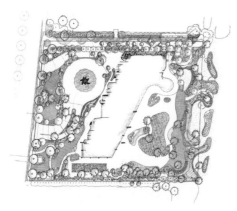

JADE SIGNATURE
Sunny Isles Beach, Florida
In conjunction with Fortune International, Herzog & de Meuron,
Pierre-Yves Rochon, and Aquadynamics

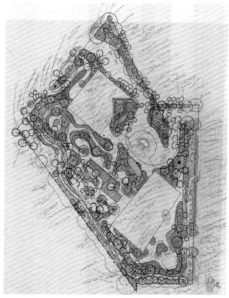

GROVE AT GRAND BAY
Coconut Grove, Florida
In conjunction with Terra Group and the
Bjarke Ingels Group (Big)

RAYMOND JUNGLES, INC.
HONORS & AWARDS

2014
Residential Design Award of Honor | National ASLA Professional
    Awards Program | Sky Garden
Award of Merit| Florida Chapter, ASLA | Pavilion Beach Club

2013
Award of Honor| Florida Chapter, ASLA | Golden Rock Inn
Award of Honor| Florida Chapter, ASLA | Sky Garden
Landscapes and Gardens Typology Award | Architizer A+ Award |
    1111 Lincoln Road

2012
Award of Excellence in Landscape Architecture | Miami Chapter,
    AIA|1111 Lincoln Road
Award of Honor | Florida Chapter, ASLA | Miami Beach Modern
    Garden
Award of Honor | Jacksonville Chapter, AIA | Refugio do Gatao
    Garden

2011
City of Miami Beach Beautification Award | 1111 Lincoln Road
City of Miami Beach Certificate of Appreciation | Miami Beach
    Botanical Garden
Award of Excellence | Florida Chapter, ASLA | 1111 Lincoln Road
Award of Honor |Florida Chapter, ASLA | Brazilian Garden
Award of Honor | Florida Chapter, ASLA | Coconut Grove, FL
    Garden

2010
Award of Excellence | Florida Nursery, Growers and Landscape
    Association | Brazilian Garden
Award of Excellence | Florida Chapter, ASLA | Brazilian Modern
    Orchid Show
Award of Merit | Florida Chapter, ASLA | The Davids Garden

2009
Award of Excellence | Florida Nursery, Growers and Landscape
    Association | Gretchen's Garden
Environmental Improvement Grand Award | The Professional
    Landcare Network | River Hammock House

2008
Frederic B. Stresau Award of Excellence | Florida Chapter, ASLA |
    Stone Reef House Garden
Award of Excellence | Florida Chapter, ASLA | Stone Reef House
    Garden
Award of Honor |Florida Chapter, ASLA | Grovenor Rooftop
    Garden
Award of Merit | Florida Chapter, ASLA | Anagrethel & Samuel
    Lewis Garden
Power Players |Florida International Magazine | People of Like
    Mind
Stars of Design Award | Design Center of the Americas |
    Landscape Design

2007
Award of Honor | Florida Chapter, ASLA | Cornfeld Garden
National ASLA Design Awards Juror

2006
Elected Fellow of the American Society of Landscape Architects

2005
Residential Design Award of Honor | National ASLA Professional
    Awards Program | Island Modern
Frederic B. Stresau Award of Excellence | Florida Chapter, ASLA
    Island Modern
Award of Excellence | Florida Chapter, ASLA | Island Modern
Award of Honor | Florida Chapter, ASLA | Casa Morada

2004
Award of Excellence | Florida Chapter, ASLA | Hyatt Windward
    Point Resort
Award of Merit | Florida Chapter, ASLA | Bergeron Garden

2003
Landscape Architect of the Year | Miami Chapter, American
    Institute of Architects (AIA)

2002
Award of Merit | Florida Chapter, ASLA | Spanish Tropical Garden
Award of Merit | Florida Chapter, ASLA | Montifiore Garden

2001
Frederic B. Stresau Award of Excellence | Florida Chapter, ASLA
    | Dunn Garden
Award of Excellence | Florida Chapter, ASLA | Dunn Garden
Award of Excellence | Florida Chapter, ASLA | Swerdlow Garden
Award of Recognition | Florida Chapter, ASLA | Lectures

2000
University of Florida Distinguished Alumnus | University of
    Florida

1998
Award of Excellence | Florida Chapter, ASLA | Salinero Garden
Award of Merit | Florida Chapter, ASLA | Marquesa Hotel

1997
Frederic B. Stresau Award of Excellence | Florida Chapter, ASLA |
    Hyatt Sunset Harbor Resort
Award of Excellence | Florida Chapter, ASLA | Hyatt Sunset
    Harbor Resort
Award of Merit | Florida Chapter, ASLA | Paradise Inn

1996
Award of Excellence | Florida Chapter, ASLA | Sims Garden
Award of Excellence | Florida Chapter, ASLA | Coral Gables
    Garden

1995
Award of Honor | Florida Chapter, ASLA | Neukomm Residence
Award of Honor | Florida Chapter, ASLA | Worrell Enterprises
Award of Excellence | Florida Chapter, ASLA | Landes Garden
Award of Excellence | Florida Nursery, Growers and Landscape
    Association | Ocean Reef Club
Environmental Improvement Grand Award | American Landscape
    Contractors Association | Ocean Reef Club

1992
Award of Excellence | Florida Chapter, ASLA | Coconut Beach
    Resort Hotel
Gold Award | American Resort Development Association |
    Coconut Beach Resort Hotel

1991
Award of Excellence | Florida Chapter, ASLA | Jungles/Yates
    Garden

1987
Community Design Award | Florida Chapter, ASLA | Eagle Creek
    Country Club

1981
Graduation with Honors | Bachelor of Landscape Architecture |
    University of Florida

ACKNOWLEDGMENTS

I am very fortunate to have several individuals who regularly influence my life both professionally and personally. Many have contributed to the development of my practice and over three decades of built work.

It is an absolute joy to share these pages with my clients who impart me with their trust and who show enthusiasm for the design process. To the many consistent consultants and contractors who pushed the envelope to engineer and built the systems needed to realize the designs.

The aptitude to visualize and articulate my designs is credited to "maestros" Roberto Burle Marx, Lawrence Halprin, Frederick Law Olmsted, and Luis Barragán, among others.

My life was greatly enriched by the generosity of Roberto Burle Marx. It was a great privilege to be able to share his routine of life. I received a lifetime of inspiration. I feel his presence every day and my senses are constantly stimulated by his art.

To my studio of past and present creatives who provided long-term support in the design, management and construction of these gardens. Thank you for your dedication and contributions to the projects and to the culture of the studio.

To my daughter, Amanda Eva Jungles, who was my in-house curator of this monograph. Without her efforts, this book would not have been possible. She has been my most ardent fan.

I am grateful to the Monacelli Press, Gianfranco Monacelli, Elizabeth White, Stacee Lawrence, Michael Vagnetti, and John Clifford of Think Studio. Stacee polished the narratives and worked with John to articulate a brilliant layout. I would also like to extend a special thank you to Charles Birnbaum for his elegant foreword.

To the many photographers who brilliantly captured our gardens—whereby the colors, the textures and the value of the garden spaces read in print as well as they would in person.

Over my thirty-plus years of practice, certain clients and architects have become mentors, colleagues and trusted friends. I would like to thank them for their sound advice and constructive criticisms; a special thank you to Bob Davids for his generosity and wisdom. I most assuredly could not have sustained such growth if it were not for the power behind his words.

To my talented wife, Gina De Souza Jungles, for being supportive despite the many weekends spent designing under the immense pressure of deadlines. She is my sounding board and she has comforted me during my studio's growing pains. It is a great joy sharing my life with you.

This book is dedicated in loving memory of my mother, Leelah Jungles. She activated my inspirations.

Marion Brenner: Collage page (row three right) 73, 77, 102 (bottom right), 108, 114 (bottom left), 115, 116 (right), 120, 122 (middle/book spine), 197, 199, 200, 202 (left), 203

Talisman Brolin: 182

Steven Brooke: Index (middle), Collage page (top left, bottom right) 17, 22, 27, 28, 30, 31, 32, 35, 36, 37, 38, 39, 40, 41, 58, 59 (left), 60, 61, 74, 75, 80, 86 (top), 90, 94, 95, 96, 97, 98, 102 (top right, bottom left), 106, 107, 109, 132, 134, 135, 136, 137, 164, 167, 168, 170, 171 (left), 172, 173, 190 (left and middle), 204, 206, 208, 209

Stephen Dunn :Inside Title Page, Index (far right), Collage page (row two and three right, row one and two left), 10, 14, 15, 16, 18, 19, 20, 21, 26, 29, 42, 44, 46, 47, 48, 49, 62, 66, 67, 68, 69, 70, 78, 79, 82, 84, 85, 86 (bottom), 87, 88, 89, 110, 116 (left), 117, 118, 119, 121, 122 (top left, top middle, bottom), 124, 127, 128 (left), 129, 130, 131, 138, 141, 142, 143, 144, 145, 146, 147, 148, 149, 150, 151, 152, 156, 157, 158, 159, 160, 161, 162, 163, 174, 178, 179, 180, 181, 188, 191, 192

Richard Felber:201

Roger Foley: Index (far left), 50, 54, 55, 56, 57, 59 (right), 169, 171 (right), 194, 198, 202 (right)

Robin Hill:193

Amanda Eva Jungles Photography:76, 123 (bottom)

Raymond Jungles:114 (top left), 128 (right), 186 (top left)

Patrick O'Brien Photography: 177

Erick Oeseburg Photography: 114 (right)

Annie Schlechter Photography: 102 (top left), 103, 104, 105

Dave Schroeder Photography: 123 (top)

Curtice Taylor Photography:186 (bottom left and bottom right), 187

Claudia Uribe: 65

Copyright © 2015 by The Monacelli Press, LLC.

All rights reserved.

Published in the United States by The Monacelli Press, LLC.

Library of Congress Control Number 2015938511

Printed in China

10 9 8 7 6 5 4 3 2 1
First edition

Designed by Think Studio, NYC

www.monacellipress.com